THE POWER OF TEN 2ND ED

A CONVERSATIONAL APPROACH TO TACKLING THE TOP TEN PRIORITIES IN NURSING

SUSAN B. HASSMILLER, PhD, RN, FAAN
JENNIFER S. MENSIK, PhD, RN, NEA-BC, FAAN

 Sigma Theta Tau International
Honor Society of Nursing®

The Honor Society of Nursing, Sigma Theta Tau International (STTI) is a nonprofit organization founded in 1922 whose mission is advancing world health and celebrating nursing excellence in scholarship, leadership, and service. Members include practicing nurses, instructors, researchers, policymakers, entrepreneurs and others. STTI's 509 chapters are located at 709 institutions of higher education in 28 countries, including Armenia, Australia, Botswana, Brazil, Canada, Colombia, England, Ghana, Hong Kong, Japan, Kenya, Lebanon, Malawi, Mexico, the Netherlands, Pakistan, Portugal, Singapore, South Africa, South Korea, Swaziland, Sweden, Taiwan, Tanzania, Thailand, the United Kingdom, and the United States of America. More information about STTI can be found online at www.nursingsociety.org.

Sigma Theta Tau International
550 West North Street
Indianapolis, IN, USA 46202

To order additional books, buy in bulk, or order for corporate use, contact Nursing Knowledge International at 888.NKI.4YOU (888.654.4968/US and Canada) or +1.317.634.8171 (outside US and Canada).

To request a review copy for course adoption, email solutions@nursingknowledge.org or call 888. NKI.4YOU (888.654.4968/US and Canada) or +1.317.634.8171 (outside US and Canada).

To request author information, or for speaker or other media requests, contact Marketing, Honor Society of Nursing, Sigma Theta Tau International at 888.634.7575 (US and Canada) or +1.317.634.8171 (outside US and Canada).

ISBN: 9781940446752
EPUB ISBN: 9781940446769
PDF ISBN: 9781940446776
MOBI ISBN: 9781940446783

Library of Congress Cataloging-in-Publication data

Names: Hassmiller, Susan, 1954- author. | Mensik, Jennifer, author. | Sigma Theta Tau International, issuing body.
Title: The power of ten / Susan B. Hassmiller, Jennifer S. Mensik.
Other titles: Preceded by (work): Power of ten, 2011-2013.
Description: Second edition. | Indianapolis, IN : Sigma Theta Tau International, [2017] | Preceded by The power of ten, 2011-2013 : nurse leaders address the profession's ten most pressing issues. c2011. | Includes bibliographical references and index.
Identifiers: LCCN 2016035390 (print) | LCCN 2016036787 (ebook) | ISBN 9781940446752 (print : alk. paper) | ISBN 9781940446769 (epub) | ISBN 9781940446776 (pdf) | ISBN 9781940446783 (mobi) | ISBN 9781940446769 (Epub) | ISBN 9781940446776 (Pdf) | ISBN 9781940446783 (Mobi)
Subjects: | MESH: Nursing--organization & administration | Leadership | Education, Nursing
Classification: LCC RT89 (print) | LCC RT89 (ebook) | NLM WY 105 | DDC 362.17/3068--dc23
LC record available at https://lccn.loc.gov/2016035390

First Printing, 2016

Publisher: Dustin Sullivan
Acquisitions Editor: Emily Hatch
Editorial Coordinator: Paula Jeffers
Cover Designer: Katy Bodenmiller

Development & Project Editor: Carla Hall
Copy Editor: Jane Palmer
Proofreaders: Jane Palmer and Todd Lothery
Page Design and Composition: Rebecca Batchelor

Dedications

For my mother, Jacqueline Wouwenberg, the first nurse I ever met. She never once told me to be a nurse, but through her actions of caring, passion, dedication, love of learning, equity for all, and standing up for what is right and what you believe, I never wanted to be anything else.
And to my husband, Bob, who has supported me through every step of the last 37 years to allow me to focus on my love of nursing and my obsession with finding ways for nurses to contribute and lead in our healthcare system.

–Susan Hassmiller

To all the nurses who belong to Generation X and Y: I believe in you.
I watch in amazement the great things you all have done in your dedication for nursing.
And therefore, I have great faith in what you all will continue to do for our profession tomorrow and beyond.

–Jennifer Mensik

Our share of royalties from this book will be donated equally to American Red Cross nursing programs and the American Nurses Foundation.

Table of Contents

Foreword

Our nation's healthcare system is at a crossroads. Patients are seeking easier access to care and information, with an increased concern about the high out-of-pocket costs of those services. At the same time, payors have targeted care coordination as a way to increase efficiency in the system and reduce wasteful spending. With the passage of the Affordable Care Act, the government has highlighted its desire to see the healthcare system move from one of "sick care" to a system that focuses on wellness. In addition, all stakeholders are now engaged in meaningful discussions about how to ensure and reward the quality of care, not just the quantity of services provided.

In many ways, the passage of the Affordable Care Act was just the beginning of these discussions about how to modernize our healthcare system for the benefit of all. While we have yet to identify one silver bullet for the most optimal system, one thing is clear: Nurses are well positioned to lead the way.

Nurses are there for the most intimate times in a person's life. We are there at the birth of a baby, caring for mothers on those momentous days. We are there to care for children in schools, keeping students healthy and ready to learn. We work in the private sector, ensuring healthy workplaces. We are professors and researchers, leading clinical trials to improve healthcare delivery and treatments. We use data to inform healthcare policy and practice. We counsel families when they face difficult diagnoses. We care for seniors as they age. And we provide hospice support and palliative care to patients and assistance to families when it is needed most.

Whether in our hospitals or clinics, schools or communities, businesses or academia, nurses have long been leaders in improving the coordination and quality of care while helping to make healthcare accessible and affordable, even in the most underserved areas.

With the implementation of the Affordable Care Act in full swing, nurses are leading the way to improve quality of care—getting people the right treatment at the right time while empowering them to be active participants in their healthcare. Moreover, nurses are measuring those outcomes to help guide future practice.

But, it is no secret to nurses and our allies that we can do more. The system is changing—the world is changing—and for nurses to continue to lead, we must evolve with it. That is why this book is so important. It highlights the 10 most important issues for the nursing profession to address in the coming years. It gives us the tools and framework to see where we have been, identify the challenges of the future, and then tackle them head-on.

This is a pretty heavy responsibility, but we are up to the challenge. Nurses know how to build consensus and forge unlikely partnerships. We know how to roll up our sleeves and get things done without waiting on others to take the lead. And we know how to identify the issues that are most important, focus on them, and work every day until we reach our goals. The essays in this book can help chart that course and guide the profession as it develops over the years to come. As the backbone of our nation's healthcare system, the nursing community must tackle these challenges and opportunities head-on. Our profession—and patients—depend on it.

–Congresswoman Lois Capps

Introduction

Welcome to the second edition of *The Power of Ten*. It has been 5 years since the first publication, and much has changed in the world, as well as in the profession. We received an opportunity to determine an updated list of 10 items, or themes, that the profession should focus on in guiding the future of the profession. While a plethora of important issues exists, certainly more than 10, we narrowed down a large list to the 10 themes noted in this book.

To initially determine these themes, we asked over 50 national and international nursing leaders for the top 5-10 issues they felt the profession needed to tackle in the next few years. Based on the responses received, we grouped the issues together, and categories, or themes, emerged. We chose 10 themes and invited contributors in those areas of expertise to write an essay for the corresponding theme. The themes are:

1. Educational Reform
2. Academic Progression
3. Diversity
4. Interprofessional Collaboration
5. Systems Thinking

6. Voice of Nursing
7. Global Stewardship
8. Practice Authority
9. Delivery of Care
10. Professional Handoff

To ensure diversity, we chose contributors based on expertise in the theme, in addition to race, geography, gender, and age. As nursing faces a loss of wisdom and experience from our sages, it was important to capture their perspectives on these themes while also eliciting perspectives of younger leaders in our profession. Each theme has at least two contributors—one sage and one younger leader. We gave contributors the written responses gathered from the original set of responses and then asked them to write in any direction that they, as experts, felt was appropriate. Our desire was to capture contributors' vantage points and wisdom while pushing the envelope. We wanted contributors to write about what must be done within each area for the profession to be considered successful in the near future. We consider this book a call to action.

This book is intended to be quick and to the point—each contributor writing from his or her viewpoint, incorporating different writing styles and personal experiences. While this book does not support any particular professional organization, it is difficult to remove contributors from the setting in which their expertise is derived. The reader will be able to experience and understand the wealth of work occurring in so many nursing organizations across the United States and internationally on behalf of our profession. This is why this book is so important: It is a call to action around a similar agenda, regardless of your practice setting or your country.

You will notice we have organized the book around the themed sections. As noted, each section has at least one sage and one young leader contributing separate essays. In a few sections, this structure was altered—this change will be explained in that theme's introduction. Additionally, substantial quotes from additional experts are included throughout this book to add to the rich discussion of each theme. Here is an overview of the themes with their contributors.

Educational Reform

Due to the national shortage of educators in nursing and the need for change, education was broken into two different sections: reform and progression (the next section). Heather Young of University of California, Davis and Marilyn Chow of Kaiser Permanente contribute sage advice from service and academia, and Danielle Howa Pendergrass of Eastern Utah Women's Health represents the perspective of a younger leader.

Academic Progression

Deb Trautman of the American Association of Colleges of Nursing and Pam Thompson of the American Organization of Nurse Executives represent sage advice from service and academia, while Lucia Alfano (Concordia College) represents a younger leader perspective. The contributors add to our understanding of reform within academic progression and provide readers with valuable insight.

Diversity

Beverly Malone of the National League for Nursing represents our sage leader in this section, and Adriana Perez of the University of Pennsylvania contributes a younger leader perspective. This section focuses on obtaining diversity in our workforce, including service and academia.

Interprofessional Collaboration

In this section, Brenda Zierler of the University of Washington is our sage contributor, with Stephen Perez of the University of Pennsylvania representing the younger leader perspective.

Systems Thinking

The systems thinking section focuses on the highest level perspective of our healthcare system, or lack thereof, and the necessary steps to create a functioning system. Mary Naylor of the University of Pennsylvania is our sage section contributor, and Suzanne Miyamoto of the American Association of Colleges of Nursing represents the younger leader perspective.

Voice of Nursing

Although the voice of nursing can be heard throughout the book, this section in particular focuses on how to be that voice, in any situation. Here we have national and international sage contributors Linda Burnes Bolton of Cedars-Sinai and Frances Hughes of the International Council of Nurses, as well as Jesse Kennedy of the American Nurses Association, the younger leader contributor.

Global Stewardship

The global stewardship section pushes the profession to think beyond borders. Judith Shamian of the International Council of Nurses is our sage contributor, and doctoral student Elizabeth Holguin is our younger contributor.

Practice Authority

The focus of this section is on all levels of practice; however, much of the discussion remains at the advanced practice registered nurse level. Here, our sage contributor is Margaret Flinter of Community Health Center, and our younger contributor is Garrett Chan of Stanford Health Care.

Delivery of Care

In this section, sage contributor Kathy Sanford of Catholic Health Initiatives and younger contributor Andrea Tanner of New Albany-Floyd County Schools discuss how delivery of care must change.

Professional Handoff

The professional handoff section is about mentoring, leaving a legacy, and preparing others for professional leadership. Terrie Sterling of Our Lady of the Lake Regional Medical Center is our sage contributor, and Diana Ruiz of the Medical Center Health System is our younger leadership contributor.

Afterword

Julie Fairman, PhD, RN, FAAN, a well-respected nurse historian, wrote the afterword. After reading about where our profession needs to go, and what we must do, it is important to reflect on where we have been. Those who do not know the past are doomed to repeat it.

We hope that you enjoy this book as much as we have enjoyed writing it and working with the contributors. Our vision is that this book is a call for action, with contributions that push the limits and make us extend beyond our usual perspectives to create an even grander future for our profession.

–Susan B. Hassmiller, PhD, RN, FAAN

–Jennifer Mensik, PhD, RN, NEA-BC, FAAN

Preface

Nursing's Role in Building a Culture of Health

Building a Culture of Health is a movement taking on one of the most pervasive challenges of our time: improving the health and well-being of everyone in America. A Culture of Health places well-being at the center of every aspect of life, so that *all* communities can flourish and *all* individuals thrive, regardless of race, creed, income, or location. It is built on the premise that everyone deserves to live the healthiest life possible, and nurses must play a central role to help make people and communities healthier.

In the United States, more people are older and sicker, and far too many people require complex care. The United States spends more than any other industrialized nation on healthcare (17.5% of GDP in 2014), but it experiences worse outcomes than many countries (Martin, Hartman, Benson, Catlin, National Health Expenditure Accounts Team, 2016; Squires & Anderson, 2015). Too many children are overweight or obese and are at risk of being the first generation to live shorter and sicker lives than their parents. In fact, a shocking 70% of America's young adults are too fat, too poorly educated, or too tied up in the criminal system to serve in the military (Mission Readiness, 2014).

Health is overwhelmingly affected by where a person lives, learns, works, plays, and worships—subsequently, health problems are compounded for low-income and minority populations. In communities where poverty is endemic, children often attend lower-quality schools and have fewer safe places to play and exercise, less access to healthy food, more exposure to toxins, and fewer employment options as they get older. The County Health Rankings & Roadmaps of the Robert Wood Johnson Foundation (RWJF, 2016) have consistently shown that where you live in America has significant effects on your health. While it is true that an individual can make a personal decision to become healthier, the choices we make are based on choices we have.

The United States needs to take a more integrated, comprehensive approach to health, with increased collaboration across sectors. Since community health is inextricably linked to the health of the workforce, health and health organizations need to partner with businesses to create healthier communities. They also need to form alliances with educators, faith leaders, architects, urban planners, legislators, transportation and housing officials, mayors, and others to make our communities healthier.

Nurses, the largest group of health professionals—and rated the highest on honesty and ethical standards in Gallup polls—must play a prominent role in collaborating with others to address the health needs of this country. In fact, examples abound of how nurses are and have been building a Culture of Health—from the Nurse-Family Partnership program that has enabled first-time parents to parent better to the Stephen and Sandra Sheller 11th Street Family Health Services clinic in Philadelphia, which uses a transdisciplinary approach to deliver primary care, behavioral health, dental services, and health and wellness programs.

For the past 5 years, RWJF and AARP have led the Future of Nursing: Campaign for Action, a nationwide initiative to create a healthier America through advancing the recommendations from the landmark Institute of Medicine (2011) report *The Future of Nursing: Leading Change, Advancing Health*. Advancing the recommendations has served to prepare the nursing workforce extraordinarily well to collaborate and lead efforts to build a Culture of Health.

Each of the top 10 issues has tremendous implications for what nurses need to bring to the table to build a Culture of Health, and each corresponds to the IOM recommendations. The top 10 issues underscore that while much progress has been made, more work lies ahead to enable the nursing profession to assume leadership roles in helping Americans pursue a healthier life.

Schools of nursing need to reform their education to ensure that students are prepared to work across the continuum of care and are able to address upon graduation the multifaceted factors that affect health. This includes integrating the social determinants of health into nursing school curricula. A great example is happening in Arizona, where 40 nurses will be paired with diverse nursing students and participate in a precepted clinical experience that will support underserved populations and communities. Similarly, nurses need to advance their education so that they are on more of a peer basis with other institutional and community leaders.

Additional seamless academic progression pathways will enable more nursing students to earn baccalaureate and advanced degrees. Diversity efforts must be accelerated so that our workforce reflects the population we serve, and so all nurses can provide culturally competent care. Interprofessional and cross-sector collaboration needs to become the norm, and nurses must understand the system in which they work to take full advantage of their roles and where they might have the most value.

Nurses need to speak with a unified voice that underscores the importance of creating healthy societies at community, state, national, and global levels. They must become global stewards to advance health for all. Full practice authority, both legislatively and institutionally, must be granted in all 50 states and abroad so that all RNs and APRNs can provide efficient, cost-effective access to care where people live, learn, work, play, and worship. Nurses similarly must be engaged in improving care delivery, so that all people receive equitable, evidence-based care.

Finally, as the baby boomer generation prepares to retire, seasoned nurses must share the skills and knowledge they have accrued over a lifetime of nursing with the next generation.

Nurses who are ready to start building a Culture of Health can examine the Action Framework (see http://www.rwjf.org/en/culture-of-health/2015/11/measuring_what_matte.html). RWJF collaborated with the RAND Corporation to develop this Action Framework to help measure progress toward achieving a Culture of Health. The Action Framework reflects a vision of health and well-being as the sum of many parts, addressing the interdependence of social, economic, physical, environmental, and spiritual factors. It is intended to generate unprecedented collaboration and chart our nation's progress toward building a Culture of Health.

The framework is meant to provide entry points that resonate with different sectors, including nursing, so they can align their work with building a Culture of Health. There are four Action Areas: "Making Health a Shared Value"; "Fostering Cross-Sector Collaboration to Improve Well-Being"; "Creating Healthier, More Equitable Communities"; and "Strengthening Integration of Health Services and Systems." Within each Action Area are drivers, which provide a set of long-term priorities for individuals and organizations across sectors to focus on, both nationally and at the community level. Each Action Area also includes a list of measures intended to provide a menu of actions all sectors can take to help build a Culture of Health and track progress. As individuals, groups, and organizations make progress in the four integrated Action Areas, RWJF believes the nation will approach an outcome of improved population health, well-being, and equity.

Many nurses will already be able to see their work reflected in the Action Framework, and it can guide future efforts and partnerships. Nurses might look at the measures under "Making Health a Shared Value" and recognize their existing partnerships with communities of faith to form health ministries that focus on providing health education, promoting well-being, and improving the health of congregations and communities. Under "Fostering Cross-Sector Collaboration," they might consider how acute care nurses, public health nurses, school nurses, and occupational nurses could band together and lead efforts to work with businesses, urban planners, city governments, and others to make their communities healthier. Under "Creating Healthier, More Equitable Communities," nurses might help to implement public smoking bans. For "Strengthening Integration of Health Services and Systems," nurses could seek to overturn restrictive scope-of-practice barriers that prevent nurse practitioners from providing access to care. The tool is not meant to be prescriptive, but rather a guide to help people think more broadly about how they might contribute to keeping themselves, others, and their communities healthier.

Many possibilities exist for nurses to get involved in building a Culture of Health. Most nurses enter the profession with the goal of healing individuals, but they now have an unprecedented opportunity to create healthier communities and improve the nation's health. Nurses must be part of this movement and leave a lasting legacy to future generations.

–Susan B. Hassmiller, PhD, RN, FAAN

References

Institute of Medicine. (2011). *The future of nursing: Leading change, advancing health*. Washington, DC: The National Academies Press. Retrieved from https://iom.nationalacademies.org/Reports/2010/The-Future-of-Nursing-Leading-Change-Advancing-Health.aspx

Martin, A. B., Hartman, M., Benson, J., Catlin, A., & National Health Expenditure Accounts Team. (2016). National health spending in 2014: Faster growth driven by coverage expansion and prescription drug spending. *Health Affairs*, *35*(1), 150–160. Retrieved from http://content.healthaffairs.org/content/35/1/150.abstract

Mission Readiness. (2014). Retreat is not an option. Retrieved from http://missionreadiness.s3.amazonaws.com/wp-content/uploads/MR-NAT-Retreat-Not-an-Option2.pdf

Robert Wood Johnson Foundation. County health rankings & roadmaps. Retrieved from http://www.countyhealthrankings.org/

Squires, D., & Anderson, C. (October 2015). U.S. health care from a global perspective: Spending, use of services, prices, and health in 13 countries. Retrieved from http://www.commonwealthfund.org/publications/issue-briefs/2015/oct/us-health-care-from-a-global-perspective

Priority #1: Educational Reform

In this section:

- Reimagining Nursing Education From the Service Point of View

- Reimagining Nursing Education From an Academic Point of View

- Nursing and STEM

- Imagining a Different Educational Path

"Consumers' need for nurses' knowledge, skills, and guidance across settings has never been greater. Half the U.S. population has at least one chronic condition. That includes children, young people, and adults of all ages, not only the growing older adult population. They need nurses who know how to save lives, but just as important, how to help them live their lives to the fullest extent possible. They need nurses who embrace the patient and family caregiver teaching role, requiring deep expertise in how to anticipate the learning needs of people from many different cultures and educational

In Priority 1: Educational Reform, the essay authors speak to the essence of nursing education itself, *what we teach*. Nursing education is a form of indoctrination into the profession. How can we ensure we are creating an even stronger profession tomorrow, 10 years from now, and even 100 years from now? What we do, or do not do, will form who we are as individual nurses and our profession as a whole.

In late 2015, the U. S. National Aeronautics and Space Administration (NASA) put out a call for applicants for astronauts. These future astronauts will be prepared for missions to travel to Mars and beyond. Prospective applicants need to have a STEM-designated degree. STEM stands for Science, Technology, Engineering, and Mathematics. At this time, a BSN degree is not on the list of STEM-designated degrees. Among all the applicants with diverse undergraduate degrees, why would an applicant with a BSN not be a great candidate for a mission to Mars?

Nurses should care about this omission that excludes nurses and nursing from important contributions and opportunities. We must solve this today for current nurses and those not yet born who will want to be on a mission to Mars in 50 years.

Educational reform is Priority 1 because it is the foundation that supports every nurse in every role. Some big questions we must ask and answer include:

1. How do we get nursing formally recognized as a STEM discipline? Should we?

2. With a sharp focus on doctorate degrees, how do we invest in nursing science? Focus on PhDs? Focus on emerging nurse scientists?

3. Who should be teaching, and is there a benefit to teaching (over grants, advanced practice)?

4. Where should a majority of clinical hours for prelicensure students occur?

5. What education should occur at undergraduate and graduate levels to create a steady pipeline of nurses for boards and leadership?

6. How do we use technology to ensure great and effective distance and online learning pedagogies?

7. What does educational funding of the future look like for prelicensure and APRN students?

8. What outcomes will we see if we reform nursing education to meet the healthcare needs of our country?

backgrounds. And the country needs nurses who understand how to improve the health of populations and promote a culture of well-being for all. To assure these competencies, we need to modernize our nursing curricula and clinical experiences. And we cannot wait years for that to happen. I firmly believe that we have to pick up the pace of change because the country needs us. Now more than ever."

–Susan C. Reinhard, PhD, RN, FAAN
Senior Vice President, AARP Public Policy Institute
Chief Strategist, Center to Champion Nursing in America

Marilyn Chow
*Vice President of National Patient
Care Services and Innovation
Kaiser Permanente*

Reimagining Nursing Education From the Service Point of View

–Marilyn P. Chow, PhD, RN, FAAN

Healthcare is evolving at an ever-faster pace, reflecting trends taking place in the world at large. The impact of technology is pervasive, often disrupting traditional models—as evidenced by Uber, online retailing, and cloud computing, to name just a few. Knowledge is growing in virtually every domain at an explosive rate, facilitated by increasing capabilities across industries to aggregate and analyze vast amounts of data. Consumers expect highly personalized products and services that precisely address their needs.

Within healthcare, technologies such as 24/7 virtual care, telehealth, and wearable sensors point to a future of care delivery that is unimaginable, bound to neither time nor place. Knowledge is rapidly expanding within increasingly specialized areas; it is impossible for any single healthcare discipline to master all information pertinent to any patient, family, or caregiver. Performance improvement and innovation generate new knowledge so quickly that best practices continually evolve. As healthcare becomes more complex, meeting the needs of patients, families, and caregivers requires reducing fragmentation and keeping them at the center of care. These developments have clear implications for nursing practice and nursing education.

The first implication is that care must be delivered by interprofessional teams. The ability to participate in and lead a multidisciplinary team is an essential skill for members of every healthcare discipline and must be developed during the educational process. Students from two or more healthcare professions learning about, from, and with each other enable effective collaboration and improved health outcomes (World Health Organization, 2010). Effective interprofessional education is an ongoing approach, rather than a one-off experience, that enables students from all disciplines to enter professional practice as members of collaborative teams.

The broad adoption of performance improvement and innovation in healthcare practice necessitates redefining education and lifelong learning. The traditional view of nursing education is that it takes place at a university and is applied in clinical settings after graduation. Becoming a lifelong learner traditionally meant developing breadth and depth of knowledge over the course of a career. However, as performance improvement becomes the norm in healthcare, effective clinical practice depends on daily learning. In addition, human-centered design principles are gaining momentum as a framework for prototyping innovative care solutions. These principles require fully partnering with patients in identifying problems and developing and testing solutions. Human-centered design reflects the fundamental nursing value of patient-centeredness and requires that nurses suspend their expert role to fully understand patient experiences. Consequently, nursing education must be the beginning of a daily discipline of learning and redesigning practice from an improvement and human-centered design perspective.

Continual performance improvement in the practice setting also necessitates that new evidence be available in nursing education as soon as it is generated. Mechanisms must be put into place for more quickly incorporating research findings into the curriculum. Nursing students must both become astute consumers of research and understand that today's evidence is tomorrow's outdated standard.

Nurses are expected to continually improve practice from an evidence base in a rapidly changing environment—and to ensure that care processes are highly reliable by assessing them and reducing variation. In contrast, a model of nursing education in which curricula and courses are updated at intervals consisting of several years implicitly suggests that nursing practice is static. This contrast may contribute to the 6-to-12 month gap between completing education and beginning proficiency in nursing practice that nursing transition programs currently seek to address.

How can education better reflect the reality that we cannot foresee the future of healthcare or nursing practice? Potential answers relate to both content and delivery. Content expertise need no longer be resident to an institution, as demonstrated in open courseware from preeminent universities such as MIT and Stanford. It is possible for students in any location to take advantage of the best learning experiences available anywhere. Local faculty members are freed to coach learners, guiding them to the best resources and providing support. Learning becomes a personalized activity directed at the common purpose of providing excellent care for individuals and communities.

Enduring core elements of nursing practice certainly exist; from the point of view of nursing practice, they include qualities such as curiosity, empathy, compassion, and resilience. Regardless of the future state of healthcare or nursing practice, these qualities will remain important. A key question is how they can be developed and nurtured during nursing education. A powerful first step may be to focus on students' needs by applying human-centered design principles to nursing education. What do students need as learners, and what solutions to their needs do they envision? This implies a shift from faculty governance to a curriculum codesigned with students, a concept that has already been applied in secondary education (Sifferlin, 2013).

Delivery of nursing education must also keep pace with the changing environment. Digitally native students experience sitting in a lecture hall to receive didactic content as inefficient at best and archaic at worst. Multiple on-demand formats—recorded lectures, course reading, online tutorials, videos, and practice tests—allow students to learn at their own speed and at convenient times. Classroom time is then devoted to activities that allow interprofessional students to learn from each other and mirror what students may do in professional practice.

Simulation is an essential pedagogical tool, and thoughtful expansion of its use addresses scarce learning resources, as well as supporting on-demand learning. Three-dimensional virtual environments, such as those in Second Life, can help alleviate the demand for clinical placements (Mattison, 2013). When simulation cannot substitute for real-world experiences, it can help orient and on-board students, easing the transition to clinical care.

What clinical care will look like in the future is unknown; the only certainty is that nursing practice will continue to evolve. The core objective of nursing education must be to prepare students to pursue excellence in nursing by continually refining their practice in response to new knowledge and technology emerging in a constantly changing healthcare environment.

References

Mattison, M. (2013, March 20). Nursing students find new opportunities in virtual world of Second Life. Retrieved from http://blog.chamberlain.edu/2013/03/20/nursing-students-find-new-opportunities-in-virtual-world-of-second-life/

Sifferlin, A. (2013, March 27). A high school where students are the teachers. *TIME*. Retrieved from http://healthland.time.com/2013/03/27/a-high-school-where-the-students-are-the-teachers/

World Health Organization. (2010). *Framework for action on interprofessional education & collaborative practice*. Geneva: Author.

Reimagining Nursing Education From an Academic Point of View

–Heather M. Young, PhD, RN, FAAN

Heather Young
Dignity Health Dean's Chair for Nursing Leadership
Dean and Professor,
Betty Irene Moore School of Nursing
Associate Vice Chancellor for Nursing
University of California, Davis

Imagine future healthcare delivery that prioritizes population health through a Culture of Health. Consumers of healthcare will drive delivery to be highly accessible, convenient, and customized appropriately to the increased diversity of our population. Healthcare will happen in community-based settings where individuals live and work, with linkages to highly specialized centers featuring concentrated, in-depth expertise and resources. Nurses will work in transdisciplinary teams and will collaborate with communities, families, and individuals to design and provide care. The source of authority in health will be democratized as anyone can access evidence. Big data at the individual and community levels will inform care, integrating electronic health records with genomic, metabolomic, and environmental data. More personalized healthcare will begin before birth and be integrated into life in general; it will be more continuous and technology-enabled and less dependent on traditional hospitals and clinics. Lines will blur between health promotion and management of chronic conditions as behavioral health, mental health, and social determinants of health achieve greater integration into healthcare delivery with disruptive forces, such as social media and mobile apps to manage illness, that enhance their presence in the field. Complex healthcare solutions will require a transdisciplinary approach that fully encompasses the preferences and needs of individuals in context of their environments, as well as other determinants of health and disease. At the same time, the next generation of nursing faculty is needed to address projected shortages.

With these changes, education must evolve by retooling nurses already in practice and preparing future nurses. In addition to clinical competencies, future nurses will have to possess exceptional leadership, flexibility, and nimbleness; cultural inclusiveness; effective communication and collaboration skills; the ability to form new kinds of coalitions, teams, and strategic partnerships; strength in the use of enabling technology; an understanding of routine improvement methods and systems engineering; an appreciation for translational research; and a strong commitment to engaging those we serve. The scope of practice of healthcare professionals will be reformed to position teams (including unlicensed colleagues) to deliver effective, high-value care.

As health systems move rapidly into new models, education lags, contributing to a gap between the competencies and skills of graduates and the new demands in practice. It is imperative to be more efficient and effective in preparing the next generation to practice, teach, discover, and lead. Content becomes dated even before graduation, so practices of lifelong learning and mentorship are even more crucial. Disruptive innovations such as Massive Open Online Courses (MOOCs) are changing assumptions about education delivery. The future of higher education hinges on creating sustainable models that optimize student-centered learning and reduce costs.

It is time to revisit ways of teaching and to apply emerging pedagogical knowledge as we prepare nurses for practice, education, policy, leadership, and research. We must partner with our professional organizations as they evaluate and build consensus on essential content for baccalaureate and graduate nursing programs (AACN, 2016; NLN, 2016). Benner and colleagues (2009) provided a compelling call for transformation in nursing education that promotes the renovation and revitalization needed.

Study for a degree in nursing should occur as part of lifelong learning, starting with health education early in life, in partnership with K-12 schools, to promote general health, encourage healthy behaviors, and inspire and recruit talented future health professionals, particularly those from underrepresented groups. This partnership with nursing schools should continue as students enter high school and benefit from career advice and encouragement to make the appropriate academic choices to position themselves for success in college. At the college and university level, nursing education must move toward more student-centered approaches to learning, taking into account individual learning style and preferences in conjunction with contemporary approaches that optimize learning. These approaches could include less lecture/in-class time and more experiential and technology-supported learning, particularly for acquisition of knowledge. Integrated case-based approaches and simulation offer the opportunity to apply and critically use foundational knowledge in situations that emphasize synthesis of information, entertaining several perspectives on the problem and solution, and require a combination of analytical skills with compassionate and ethical care. Curricula already suffer from bloated content, so decisions about priority should be made carefully and critically, with an emphasis on building the skills and motivation to continue to learn after graduation. Curricular decisions must balance foundational knowledge for the profession with health issues of highest current priority in the global and local communities. These innovations must extend to lifelong learning, engaging postgraduates.

Learning in teams is essential, focusing on topics that bring us together with common interests and issues in practice that demand multiple perspectives. Nursing programs exist on diverse campuses, providing a range of potential collaborators to grapple with important problems that threaten human health and develop potential approaches beyond health sciences, such as with nutrition, informatics, genomics, business, cultural studies, policy, and others. Improving health outcomes and healthcare's performance is a mandate, and this requires understanding system science and having the skills of implementing the principles in healthcare to build capacity for practice change.

Preparation of nursing faculty is essential for the future of the profession. For those students who want academic/research careers in health sciences, universities could design and provide an integrated undergraduate/graduate program coupled with mentorship to support this aspiration. Such programs could embrace common curricula that bring together individuals interested in PhD-DVM-RN-MD academic careers, providing opportunities to collaborate in team science and streamlining research education.

Nursing education will thrive when we put health first and are in deep partnership with the communities we serve, understanding societal and environmental forces that shape health and healthcare as well as priorities of members of society and of health delivery partners. This partnership can only enhance our ability to identify target areas for education and discovery that will provide the greatest impact and enable contributions that advance health, sustainability, and equity in our communities.

"The current practice-education gap makes educational transformation in nursing education essential and urgent. Nursing graduates need to be both test-ready and practice-ready. Program leaders will need to design clinical learning for the situated use of knowledge in nursing practice. We must abandon narrow rational-technical approaches to education and provide situated coaching in clinical reasoning across time as changes in the patient/family occur. Students must learn to practice nursing in multiple contexts."

–Patricia Benner, PhD, RN, FAAN
Professor Emerita, School of Nursing
University of California,
San Francisco

References

AACN, American Association of Colleges of Nursing. (2016). Essentials series. Retrieved from http://www.aacn.nche.edu/education-resources/essential-series

Benner, P., Sutphen, M., Leonard, V., & Day, L. (2009). *Educating nurses: A call for radical transformation*. San Francisco, CA: Jossey-Bass.

NLN, National League for Nursing. (2016). Outcomes and competencies for graduates of practical/vocational, diploma, associate degree, baccalaureate, master's, practice doctorate, and research doctorate programs in nursing. Retrieved from http://nln.lww.com/products-page/product-category/9781934758120-2

Nursing and STEM

–Danielle Howa Pendergrass, DNP, APRN, WHNP-BC

Danielle Howa
Pendergrass
*President of Eastern Utah
Women's Health, LLC*

As I volunteered for a STEM project in my son's first-grade classroom, I took a look around and could not help but ask myself the all-too-familiar question: *Is nursing at the table?*

To begin with, what is STEM? While there is not a consistent, standard definition of what constitutes a STEM profession, both at the state and federal level, the most widely accepted definition holds that STEM education is an interprofessional approach to learning where rigorous academic concepts are coupled with real-world lessons as students apply science, technology, engineering, and mathematics in contexts that make connections among school, community, work, and the global enterprise (Tsupros, Kohler, & Hallinen, 2009). This learning occurs in both formal and informal settings from preschool to postdoctorate education (Gonzalez & Kuenzi, 2012). When trying to determine what constitutes a STEM profession, most studies tend to underrepresent the total number of positions that involve STEM knowledge, including nursing.

Nurses possess the inherent characteristics of scientists, researchers, and engineers who ask big questions and determine the best ways to solve problems. What if we were to join forces across sectors and use STEM as an integrated course of action to position nursing on the forefront, starting on day one of our formal education?

Students and teachers who choose a STEM profession have increased access to scholarships and funding and have higher-paying jobs (Ryan, 2012). This means that schools and colleges that promote careers in STEM professions are also candidates for funding, which raises this question: If nursing is designated as a STEM profession, would that provide funding and impetus to resolve nurse faculty shortages? Could it provide the investment needed for our emerging PhD nurse scientists?

If nursing is recognized as a STEM profession, we automatically have a seat at the table on the first day our education begins. STEM activities encourage teamwork across all interests. We would be culturalized, along with other professions, to work in creative collaborations that transcend traditional boundaries. We would be encouraging budding nurses to work and problem-solve with budding city planners, environmental engineers, and business leaders of our future. As we continue to grow alongside other professions, we set the stage for leadership and collegiality.

If nursing is recognized as a STEM profession across the nation, would it be easier for new nurses to get a seat at the critically important decision-making tables because they had been sitting at the table since their education began? Would the dialogue and collaborative action among business, government, individuals, and organizations effortlessly evolve? With a STEM designation, how much more well-positioned would nursing be to work with other professions to build healthier communities?

Nurses need to leverage current resources and encourage innovative partnerships. Both STEM and nursing are working on diversifying workforces. Women disproportionally embody nursing, while men are overrepresented in traditional STEM careers. Both are low in representing minorities, another place where we intersect and could work together. We are working on parallel planes, and I believe it is time to join forces to give a much-needed boost to the diversity in our professions.

Nursing is the single largest interest area for females who are considering STEM professions, yet nursing is not included across the board. States can choose to recognize nursing as a STEM profession. It's time to look into your state's STEM programs and see if nursing is included. If not, advocate for your profession. If it is included, look for ways to promote it. I cannot help but hear the call of nursing—we belong here!

References

Gonzalez, H. B., & Kuenzi, J. J. (2012, November 15). Science, technology, engineering, and mathematics (STEM) education: A primer. (CRS Report No. R42642). Retrieved from http://www.stemedcoalition.org/wp-content/uploads/2010/05/STEM-Education-Primer.pdf

Ryan, C. (2012, October). Field of degree and earnings by selected employment characteristics: 2011. Retrieved from https://www.census.gov/prod/2012pubs/acsbr11-10.pdf

Tsupros, N., Kohler, R., & Hallinen, J. (2009). STEM education in Southwestern Pennsylvania: A project to identify the missing components. Retrieved from http://www.cmu.edu/gelfand/documents/stem-survey-report-cmu-iu1.pdf

Nursing education is changing rapidly to optimize learning through greater learner engagement and collaboration with other disciplines and members of the public. Whether the focus is on learning to be a nurse, advancing one's clinical and leadership expertise, or building a program of science to inform the discipline, nursing education aims to improve health for all. We have the opportunities that emerging technologies provide to deepen learning, ensure patient safety and quality, and increase capacity by working ever more effectively with our clinical partners. One primary aim is to educate a diverse and inclusive workforce that understands and responds to the needs of all people throughout the world. Another key transformation is fully integrating nursing education with research, practice, and leadership to prepare nurses with the competencies needed to make dynamic and profound improvements in health (American Association of Colleges of Nursing & Manatt Health, 2016).

–*Juliann G. Sebastian, PhD, RN, FAAN*
Dean and Professor
University of Nebraska Medical Center College of Nursing

Reference

American Association of Colleges of Nursing & Manatt Health. (2016). *Advancing healthcare transformation: A new era for academic nursing*. Washington, DC: Author.

Imagining a Different Educational Path

–Heather M. Young, PhD, RN, FAAN, and Marilyn P. Chow, PhD, RN, FAAN

Heather Young
*Dignity Health Dean's Chair for Nursing
Leadership
Dean and Professor, Betty Irene Moore
School of Nursing
Associate Vice Chancellor for Nursing
University of California, Davis*

Imagine a care delivery system in which members of the healthcare team have a common core foundation and clearly understand each other's unique role and contribution to clinical care. With the exponential growth of knowledge about health and disease, an expert team is essential. One approach to develop highly functioning transdisciplinary teams is to begin with a common undergraduate major in health sciences providing holistic foundational knowledge and prerequisites for health professionals (including communication, ethics, leadership, science and arts, public health, multicultural competencies, and social determinants of health), then differentiate into professional tracks for further education and career development as nurses, physicians, pharmacists, veterinarians, therapists, dietitians, social workers, and health system administrators.

Marilyn Chow
*Vice President of National Patient Care
Services and Innovation
Kaiser Permanente*

With a shared foundation and development of competencies that are common across the health sciences, each member has the potential to contribute at a higher level to person- and family-centered care. These majors could have early admissions agreements with graduate programs in the health sciences, streamlining progression. This model would transform generic prehealth courses, such as chemistry and biology, by focusing the learning activities on health sciences as the end target. Partners in practice could collaborate with university faculty to design learning

"Change and speed are not always second nature in academic institutions, but we take courage from the nursing leaders within health systems who innovate by the minute and share their insights and recommendations with their dean partners. What have I learned? Professional nurses need to be highly accomplished clinicians as well as technology and data experts to provide high-quality, cost-effective care. Professional nurses need to not only care for the individual patient but seek information about the social determinants within the patient's community and home environment that contribute to their health or to their disease. Professional nurses must be vigilant about applying their knowledge to planning care within a cultural and community-sensitive framework. Learning these skills and competencies is a partnership; the academic environment provides the knowledge, science, and practice, and the clinical environment provides the experience."

–Bobbie Berkowitz, PhD, RN, FAAN
Dean and Professor
Columbia University School of Nursing
Sr. Vice President, Columbia University Medical Center

activities that bring to life the foundational knowledge, with opportunities to be engaged in healthcare settings and with contemporary dilemmas and challenges important in healthcare delivery. This major could form a sense of community that, when coupled with mentorship and pipeline programs, could dramatically enhance diversity in the health professions.

The clinical and health professional education could then focus on intensive clinical experience and professional role development. These intensive clinical experiences could be designed in two phases. The first phase would provide core knowledge for the chosen professional role. The second phase would focus on transdisciplinary experiences in elective areas of emphasis, such as by population (pediatrics, women's health, gerontological nursing), by setting (hospital, ambulatory care, long-term care), or across the care continuum. Both phases would be designed and implemented in partnership with health delivery systems, bringing together expert practitioners as mentors and faculty in collaboration with the university- or college-based faculty.

"How will we anticipate what nurses of the future must know and do? Reform in nursing education begins first and foremost with putting students in the center of learning. Measure competence, not clinical hours or time spent in class, and redesign using evidence, not traditions that have no scientific basis (like GPA). If we don't innovate, the gap between practice and education will mushroom. Finally, the ultimate measure of successful transformation in nursing education is graduating more nurses at all educational levels who can unlearn, relearn, and lead change."

–Jan Jones-Schenk, DHSc, RN, NE-BC
National Director, College of Health Professions
Western Governors University

Priority #2: Academic Progression

In this section:

- Transforming a Nursing Curriculum Will Help Improve Societies

- Academic Progression in Nursing

- Moving Toward a Preferred Future in Nursing

Academic progression is often grouped together with *educational reform*; however, we believed each topic is significant enough to warrant separate sections. While closely related, the profession needs deep conversation in both of these areas to secure solid forward movement.

As you read through Priority 2: Academic Progression, think about the following statements and questions. While our essay authors did not need to address these specific questions or issues, we offered them as a guide in exploring the topic. If you were to think radically outside of the box, what would your answers be?

1. How do we promote clinical immersion experiences for APRN students and expedited BSN to PhD and DNP educational pathways?

2. We are making small progress on the nation's BSN percentage. How do we make the BSN the nursing preparation for entry into practice?

3. Is it time to take the best of the best plans for academic progression and go with it?

4. How, as a profession, do we address issues and concerns over the quality of RN to BSN programs?

5. If the profession was to resolve all academic progression issues, what would it look like 10 years from now?

6. How do we direct more undergraduate students to a career in research, science, and innovation through the PhD degree?

" A cultural shift is happening in the landscape of nursing. Nurses rarely speak of 'entry into practice' as they once did with heated debate. Instead, we speak about 'academic progression in nursing,' with the goal of 80% of nurses achieving the bachelor's degree by 2020. We need *all* nurses, regardless of their entry into practice, to continue their educational journey to the BSN or higher with employers' robust support. Nurses recognize the need for the best patient outcomes possible, more nurse educators, more nurses to fill the places retired nurses will vacate, more nurses to care for baby boomers, more nurses to care for those with better access to healthcare, and more nurses to serve the global needs of humankind. This is a call to action: Embrace the cultural shift of academic progression in nursing! "

–*Kathryn Tart, EdD, MSN, RN*
Founding Dean and Professor
University of Houston School of Nursing

Lucia Alfano
Nursing Faculty
Concordia College, New York
Public Health Nurse, Sterling Home
Care, Connecticut

Transforming a Nursing Curriculum Will Help Improve Societies

–Lucia J. Alfano, MA, RN

When I began studying for my associate's degree in nursing (ADN), I had no idea what I was getting myself into. Nor did I know all of what nursing meant. What I did know was that for me to escape a world of poverty, I would have to get an education. My primary education had been up to sixth grade. I went from sixth grade to taking a high school equivalency test and then straight to a community college. In community college, I learned the art of caring and dived right into a world of lifelong learning.

When entering nursing courses, I realized that support and tutoring for students were lacking. There was also minimal conversation about moving on to a baccalaureate program. At that time (2000), academic progression or the transition from a junior college to a senior college was not deemed as important as it is today. This served as motivation for me to establish a student peer-to-peer mentoring/tutoring program, a fully student-led, first-of-its-kind initiative that would help nursing students for years to come.

Transitioning to a baccalaureate (BSN) program was an overwhelming journey for me. I realize now that the transition from ADN to BSN did not need to be as hard. Today, we have programs such as articulation agreements and mentoring programs that help students through this transition. Still, these programs are not standardized, and it is not well known which colleges have them and which do not.

Academic progression is not standard practice throughout the nation. For example, fewer than a dozen states are mandated by law to have an articulation agreement, while other states do it on a voluntary basis—although evidence is clear that this is a successful pathway to progression in nursing education. These programs help students experience an easier transition from community colleges to senior colleges.

Other process measures that have proven to help students succeed in nursing education are mentoring programs, supportive and culturally sensitive resources, career counseling, and bringing education onto employment premises. Still, students are not always aware of which institutions have these amenities. We need to have this kind of information accessible in one place and under one site. We need a reliable national hub where we can store resources of academic progression for our nursing students to access and for our academic institutions to replicate.

As we pursue having the BSN become the entry-level degree for nurses, we mustn't devalue an ADN-prepared nurse. However, to avoid duplication, decrease costs, facilitate success, and promote interprofessional education, we must look to a future of combining ADN and BSN curricula. ADN and BSN programs have the potential to come together within the same bricks and mortar. Prioritizing

"When you are deciding if it's the right time to go forward and advance your degree, follow your heart, dreams, and passion wherever they might take you. Some may try to tell you what that should look like, but don't be afraid to do it on your own time. Whether that's after 30 years or after 1 year, it's your journey. That's the beauty of nursing: There is no one path forward. You will be the one doing the work throughout the program, and you will be the one doing the work after you graduate from the program. So if it's the right time for *you*, go for it!"

–Kelly Haight
MSN, APRN, ACNS-BC, PCCN
Clinical Nurse Specialist
Cleveland Clinic

nursing and public health lessons from the very beginning will prepare nurses for our changing practice arena. Helping students obtain RN licensure and awarding them an ADN halfway through should be made possible. Models like this work for other disciplines and carry much possibility in academic progression for nursing education evolvement.

I became nursing faculty because of my immense desire to improve societies. I knew in my heart that the improvements I could contribute to nursing education could put me on the right path toward this goal. At the core of building improved societies is preparing health professionals to develop this same aspiration. As a leader, mentor, and educator, I am able to do this for many. I envision myself as a future nurse scientist who will revolutionize the way we educate and practice the art of caring. Developing interprofessional curriculums that will bring multiple health disciplines together will be the focus of my future in academia.

Implementing interprofessional and standardized models to support academic progression in nursing needs urgent attention. To accomplish this, nursing programs need to intentionally open their minds and curriculums to new opportunities. We need to do this together, without fear of ridicule or failure. We can learn together and develop efficient programs that will help our students through a transition that can be daunting. Nursing education curricula need an overhaul. This will support our population's changing demographics and the transformation of healthcare delivery systems.

Academic Progression in Nursing

–Pamela Thompson, MS, RN, CENP, FAAN

The Robert Wood Johnson Foundation's Academic Progression in Nursing (APIN) grant was awarded to the Tri-Council of Nursing (American Association of Colleges of Nursing [AACN], American Nurses Association [ANA], American Organization of Nurse Executives [AONE], and National League for Nursing [NLN]) in 2012. The National Program Office for the grant is located at AONE as the organization served as the administrator of the grant for Tri-Council. The overall goal of APIN was to provide assistance to nine state action coalitions to implement the Institute of Medicine recommendation that 80% of the nursing workforce have a bachelor of science in nursing (BSN) by 2020.

The nine states became a living laboratory, testing four promising models to achieve a better educated workforce. They began to identify strategies that worked, as well as strategies that did not achieve the goal. There was also an intent to identify which strategies could be scaled up and used by other states to meet the 2020 goal. The nine states were California, Hawaii, Massachusetts, Montana, New Mexico, New York, North Carolina, Texas, and Washington.

Pamela Thompson
Chief Executive Officer
American Organization of Nurse Executives
Senior Vice President for Nursing
Chief Nursing Officer
American Hospital Association

"As the healthcare system in the United States continues to undergo transformation, so must the educational system of the nursing profession. Academic progression is imperative for all levels of nursing to facilitate the provision of optimal healthcare in our communities. Unique models of academic progression are a driving force for baccalaureate nursing education. Community colleges play a key role in educating the nursing workforce. They should have the opportunity to confer the bachelor of science in nursing or partner with a university so that all communities have access to baccalaureate-prepared nurses and opportunities for continued academic progression. This is nursing's time in history to be unified and demonstrate the ultimate concern for positive health outcomes."

–Donna Meyer, MSN, RN, ANEF
Chief Executive Officer
Organization for Associate Degree Nursing

The four models tested are:

1. **RN to BSN degrees conferred by community colleges:** Currently, only seven community colleges can confer the baccalaureate. Although this could accelerate the achievement of an increased BSN-prepared workforce, it does not appear to offer sufficient capacity.

2. **Accelerated options of RN to MSN programs:** This option allows nurses with an associate degree in nursing (ADN) to move quickly to advanced practice, achieving a BSN in the process. More popular, however, are the accelerated RN to BSN options, which are offered by many of the online programs.

3. **State and regional shared competency or outcome-based curriculum:** This strategy focuses on a curriculum that defines the level of competency students must achieve and demonstrate in their clinical and professional outcomes.

4. **Shared statewide or regional curriculum:** This model requires a consensus and partnership among schools to develop a shared curriculum. This strategy enhances seamless progression and reduces duplication of courses for students.

The four models have proved to be promising strategies, in various degrees. But, none of the four in and of itself will be able to achieve the 80% goal by 2020. It is becoming clear that, based on the APIN work with the four, a fifth model is showing significant promise.

This new model is based on the shared statewide or regional curriculum strategy (#4). Some components include dual enrollment by the student in both the community college and the university at the beginning of study, seamless transition for the student with no duplication of courses, and shared resources between community colleges and universities. Both an ADN and BSN are conferred, but the student does not exit the program until the BSN requirements are completed. These programs are allowing students to complete their studies faster. It benefits both the community college and the university, as both confer their degrees.

Additional learnings from the work of the states are the "readiness factors" that must be present for these initiatives to be successful. These include:

1. Good relationships among the involved parties, especially community colleges and universities, and those responsible for the success of the program. Grantees that have progressed the fastest have built on relationships that have been years in the making.

2. Leadership from individuals and organizations in the form of time, money, and personnel. This includes the need for a dedicated champion to guide the work.

3. Supportive infrastructures with dedicated individuals who organize and execute the plans.

4. Sustainability plans are critical. These must include how the work will be institutionalized after the grant money goes away.

5. Competencies of individuals working on the plans include knowledge and expertise in change management, innovation, systems thinking, complexity science, and organizational behavior.

6. Strong partnerships among academic and practice communities are critical.

These readiness factors make it possible to create initiatives that are productive, sustainable, and scalable to increase the number of BSN members of the workforce.

Most important is the presence of a robust academic/practice partnership. APIN states where this partnership is strong have made the most progress. Issues critical for nurse leaders include the following:

1. Practice represents the locale for members of the incumbent workforce, and they, too, should be encouraged to progress to their BSN if we are to achieve

the 80% goal. Nurse leaders can set this expectation within their facilities so that the nurses understand that it is a goal.

2. Nurse leaders in practice can support their staff with employment benefits such as tuition reimbursement, schedule flexibility, and other personnel policies that facilitate going back to school.

3. Nurse leaders are well aware of where the future practice is headed and can see firsthand where education may need to change to meet future demands. They must take an active role to work with their academic partners as these changes emerge to make sure the curriculum stays current and future-focused.

4. Nurse leaders can be valuable partners if they are included in APIN work from the beginning of the initiative. APIN states that did not include practice partners from the beginning are realizing that their progress may be slowed without it. Nurse leaders should discuss workforce education needs with their local academic colleagues and encourage partnerships to achieve educational progression in the workplace.

5. Nurse leaders do not want to be told what to do, nor do they want to be passive recipients of expectations. Defining the attributes of what a practice/academic partnership can be is work for both parties.

6. It is critical that practice leaders be strong advocates for academic progression within their facilities. They must be able to articulate the return on investment for a better educated workforce. It is their voice that can assure the achievement of better-educated nurses.

Our future ability to accelerate academic progression is dependent on a close relationship between education and practice. Neither can address our future in isolation. Both need to be involved in designing education needs for our future nurses and our incumbent workforce. Working together, we can design and implement a seamless system that assures congruence between how we educate nurses and how practice will evolve in an ever-changing healthcare environment. I call on all nurse leaders to join the work to accomplish this. It is critical for our profession that they do so.

"We need to move past the decades-old debate about the educational preparation of nurses. The public expects and deserves nurses who are prepared to practice in an increasingly complex healthcare system. For this reason, the nursing profession must set clear academic preparation criteria and facilitate mechanisms for current and future nurses to achieve those standards. Furthermore, nurses—individually and collectively—should embrace the concept of academic progression as a professional expectation and responsibility."

–Jean Giddens, PhD, RN, FAAN
Dean and Professor
Doris B. Yingling Endowed Chair
Virginia Commonwealth University School of Nursing
Robert Wood Johnson Foundation
Nurse Executive Fellow Alumna

Deborah Trautman
President and Chief Executive Officer
American Association of Colleges of
Nursing (AACN)

Moving Toward a Preferred Future in Nursing

–*Deborah E. Trautman, PhD, RN, FAAN*

"A more highly educated nursing profession is no longer a preferred future; it is a necessary future in order to meet the nursing needs of the nation and to deliver effective and safe care" (Tri-Council, 2010, para. 8).

This call to action from the Tri-Council for Nursing's 2010 policy statement on the educational advancement of registered nurses echoes a growing consensus within the larger healthcare arena for moving the nursing workforce further along the educational continuum. Entry-level preparation is only the first step in a nurse's professional formation; embracing lifelong learning is today's norm. Nurse educators at all levels recognize this new "mandate." In the Joint Statement on Academic Progression for Nursing Students and Graduates, endorsed by national leaders representing registered nursing (RN) programs in both community colleges and universities in 2012, all were united in the view that full support must be given to nurses pursuing higher levels of education.

Support for academic progression—a key recommendation in the 2010 Institute of Medicine (IOM) report *The Future of Nursing: Leading Change, Advancing Health*—is now widely embraced by most organizations, employers, and opinion leaders interested in moving the profession forward. The Affordable Care Act

(ACA) was passed the year prior to the IOM report. The ACA advanced new models of care delivery that expand opportunities for nursing practice. As leaders of health/medical homes, nurse-managed health clinics, community health centers, and other settings, nurses are moving to become full partners in driving change in the healthcare arena. As more patients enter the system and an aging population creates the demand for transformation in healthcare, many more nurses will soon be serving in primary care and specialty roles, as well as leading independent practices. All of these exciting new developments underscore the need for a more highly educated nursing workforce.

Additionally, the evidence-based findings in the IOM report present a clear argument for facilitating national, state, and local efforts to advance the formal education of today's RN in the interest of advancing patient safety. Groundbreaking research from Linda Aiken (2003, 2008, 2014), Olga Yakusheva (2014), Mary Blegen (2013), and others underscores the link between baccalaureate-level nursing education and lower mortality rates, shorter lengths of stay, and other positive care outcomes.

Long before the IOM report and Aiken's landmark study in *JAMA*, the American Association of Colleges of Nursing (AACN) had advocated for the creation of a more highly educated nursing workforce as the key to providing quality care and protecting patients. As academic nursing leaders, we understand that education matters and has a direct impact on a nurse's ability to provide essential services along the continuum of care.

"It is essential to keep academic progression in the minds and futures of nursing students from the day they enter nursing school. With an improving job market for new graduates—yes, a widespread nursing shortage is approaching—healthcare employers will find it more difficult to recruit BSN graduates and will hire all ADNs. There may or may not be a stipulation that new hires advance their education, especially if tuition reimbursement is not part of the employment benefits package. Delivery of high quality patient care and access to superior nursing services require that RNs meet this expectation through academic progression and continuing education."

–Diane Mancino, EdD, RN, CAE, FAAN
Executive Director
National Student Nurses' Association Inc.

In response to this growing body of evidence and widespread support for baccalaureate-level nursing education, hospitals and health systems are changing how they do business, including the type of nurse they hire to provide front-line care. Data collected by the AACN (October 2015) show that 79% of employers are now requiring or expressing a strong preference for nurses with a bachelor's degree.

Nursing schools are being responsive to market demands and the IOM recommendation for an 80% baccalaureate-prepared nursing workforce by 2020 by expanding their portfolios of entry-level and degree-completion programs. Since the publication of the IOM report in 2010, 63 new entry-level bachelor of science in nursing (BSN) programs have opened nationwide, bringing the total number of these programs in the United States to 656. For practicing nurses wishing to complete a BSN, 594 programs are now available, including 46 new programs that have opened in the last 5 years. For individuals with degrees in other fields who wish to transition into nursing, 299 accelerated BSN programs are the preferred pathway into the profession. Finally, for those wishing to accelerate their education to the master's level (MSN), 209 RN-to-MSN degree-completion programs and 63 entry-level MSN programs are available to prospective students (AACN, 2015).

Given the dramatic increase in the number of baccalaureate-level nursing programs enrolling students, the need to maintain academic rigor in these offerings is growing in importance. With the sharpest increase in degree-completion programs, AACN issued a white paper on *Expectations for Practice Experiences in the RN to Baccalaureate Curriculum* in 2012 to provide guidance to schools and students on how to assess program quality and ensure a new level of competency for graduates. Increasing educational options without maintaining high quality standards will not serve the profession or the public.

In terms of achieving higher levels of education, our progress is beginning to show. For more than a decade, enrollment in BSN programs has increased steadily each year. After the IOM recommended a near-doubling of the number of baccalaureate-prepared nurses in the workforce, the number of students entering these programs accelerated rapidly. Over the last 5 years, enrollment in RN-to-BSN programs increased by 69%, and enrollment in entry-level BSN programs increased by 17%. Despite these gains, only about 55% of the RN population is currently prepared at the baccalaureate or higher degree level, according to the latest numbers available from the National Council of State Boards of Nursing (Budden, Zhong, Moulton, & Cimiotti, 2013).

Reaching the IOM goal related to baccalaureate preparation will require innovative solutions and collective action among all parties engaged in the development of future generations of nurses. Now is the time for nurse educators, higher education administrators, employers, legislators, and other stakeholders to commit to marshalling resources and providing opportunities to enable all nurses to take the next step in their educational development.

AACN strongly believes in the power of collaboration, and we look forward to continuing to work with all stakeholders to better prepare nurses to lead and transform care across roles and practice settings by advancing their education to the baccalaureate and graduate degree level. Together we can send a clear message that quality nursing education matters, while instilling a passion for lifelong learning among new recruits to the profession.

References

Aiken, L. (2014, October). Baccalaureate nurses and hospital outcomes: More evidence. *Medical Care, 52*(10), 861–863.

Aiken, L. H., Clarke, S. P., Cheung, R. B., Sloane, D. M., & Silber, J. H. (2003, September 24). Educational levels of hospital nurses and surgical patient mortality. *Journal of the American Medical Association, 290,* 1617–1623.

Aiken, L. H., Clarke, S. P., Sloane, D. M., Lake, E. T., & Cheney, T. (2008, May). Effects of hospital care environment on patient mortality and nurse outcomes. *Journal of Nursing Administration, 38*(5), 223–229.

American Association of Colleges of Nursing. (2012). Expectations for practice experiences in the RN to baccalaureate curriculum. Retrieved from http://www.aacn.nche.edu/aacn-publications/white-papers/RN-BSN-White-Paper.pdf

American Association of Colleges of Nursing. (2015). *2014-2015 enrollment and graduations in baccalaureate and graduate programs in nursing.* Washington, DC: Author.

American Association of Colleges of Nursing. (2015, October). Employment of new nurse graduates and the employment of baccalaureate-prepared nurses. Retrieved from http://www.aacn.nche.edu/leading_initiatives_news/news/2015/employment15

American Association of Colleges of Nursing, American Association of Community Colleges, Association of Community College Trustees, National League for Nursing, National Organization for Associate Degree Nursing. (2012, September). Joint statement on academic progression for nursing students and graduates. Retrieved from http://www.aacn.nche.edu/aacn-publications/position/joint-statement-academic-progression

Blegen, M. A., Goode, C. J., Park, S. H., Vaughn, T., & Spetz, J. (2013, February). Baccalaureate education in nursing and patient outcomes. *Journal of Nursing Administration, 43*(2), 89–94.

Budden, J. S., Zhong, E. H., Moulton, P., & Cimiotti, J. P. (2013, July 13). The National Council of State Boards of Nursing and The Forum of State Nursing Workforce Centers 2013 National Workforce Survey of Registered Nurses. *Journal of Nursing Regulation, 4*(2), S1–S72.

Institute of Medicine. (2010). *The future of nursing: Leading change, advancing health.* Washington, DC: National Academies Press.

Tri-Council for Nursing. (2010, May). Educational advancement of registered nurses: A consensus position. Retrieved from http://www.aacn.nche.edu/Education/pdf/TricouncilEdStatement.pdf

Yakusheva, O., Lindrooth, R., & Weiss, M. (2014, October). Economic evaluation of the 80% baccalaureate nurse workforce recommendation: A patient-level analysis. *Medical Care, 52*(10), 864–869.

"It is imperative that academic institutions offering the baccalaureate and higher degrees in nursing be truly committed to have smoother transitions for the nonbaccalaureate-prepared nurse. This requires that we think outside the box and create innovative programs that adhere to the standards set by our accrediting bodies and the profession. The complexity of healthcare requires that we have the best qualified nurses leading the change in how patients, families, and communities can restore health, protect their health, maintain their health, and promote their health. Now is the time to seize this opportunity and be bold and audacious in this venture."

–Catherine Alicia Georges, EdD, RN, FAAN
Professor and Chairperson
Department of Nursing, Lehman College

Priority #3: Diversity

In this section:

- Diversity and Meaningful Inclusion

- Progress and Challenges in Growing a Diverse Nursing Workforce

It is essential that we not only improve diversity, but also resolve any issues within our profession if we are going to have an impact those we care for. Issues relating to diversity in nursing include:

- The large aging population has implications for primary care and specialty care that need to be met with specialists in nursing.

- Healthcare disparities continue to affect the quality of health and care among populations with racial, ethnic, socioeconomic, sexual, and gender diversity.

- Despite an increasingly diverse U.S. population, the nursing workforce does not yet represent this diversity.

- With the increased diversity of the U.S. population, cultural competence must include being aware of, as well as responding to, the values and beliefs of those we care for that are different from those of the nurse.

Inclusion and equity within our profession include all levels of students, from entry level to advanced practice, and all future nurse scientists and educators. The profession cannot address our future if we do not resolve our culture clashes.

What do we need to do, and what can we do in the near future?

1. How do we significantly increase diversity in nursing—from service to academia?

2. How do we create a workforce that is diverse, educated, and socialized to see health as part of the continuum?

3. How do we actively recruit and then provide financial support for education that targets racial and ethnic groups currently underrepresented in nursing?

4. How do we connect health and social systems to align with the needs of an increasingly diverse population?

5. How do we address all types of diversity and inclusion, such as baby boomers, older adults, students, immigrants—all generations and geographies?

As you read through the essays, how will you take their thoughts and your ideas and put them into a practice that leads to meaningful change?

"Regardless of life's circumstance, diversity creates a colorful mosaic in which all the colors are equal, reminding us that the mosaic of diversity is the intersection where human dignity and difference meet."

–*Barbara L. Nichols, DNSc (hon), MS, RN, FAAN*
Visiting Associate Professor
University of Wisconsin-Madison
College of Nursing
Diversity Coordinator
Wisconsin Center for Nursing

Beverly Malone
Chief Executive Officer
National League for
Nursing (NLN)

Diversity and Meaningful Inclusion

–Beverly Malone, PhD, RN, FAAN

I grew up in a household where I had lighter skin color than my mother or father. My mother tells me that when she would take me out, our neighbors would ask, "Whose baby is that?" implying that I couldn't be hers since her color was so much darker than mine. So I grew up waiting for summer so the sun could bake me a beautiful rich black color, and no one would know my secret until winter washed the color away. I was averse to lotion because I thought it might make me lighter. It was the reassuring voice of my great-grandmother—Ms. Addie, the community healer—that helped me begin understanding the lovely bouquet of colors that African-American people possessed. As I grew older, I began to realize and reflect: Maybe there's diversity in everyone's family, not just mine. Perhaps it's universal that we struggle with the idea of differences and uniqueness. Perhaps it's beautiful that we consciously struggle with our differences and embrace and celebrate those, as well as unconsciously relax and rest in our similarities. We are always assured that we are more similar than different.

The National League for Nursing (NLN, n.d.) defines diversity as "affirming the uniqueness of and differences among persons, ideas, values, and ethnicities" (para. 1). The unique and individual differences usually identified include race, ethnicity, gender, sexual orientation and gender identity, socioeconomic status, age, physical abilities, religious beliefs, political beliefs, or other attributes. We are nurses, and our code of ethics demands that we provide care to all—that we understand that diversity, meaningful inclusion, and quality healthcare are inseparable. This is non-negotiable as a nurse. This understanding cannot just be conceptual but has to be operational in the care, healing, teaching, and leading that we provide.

The challenging part is to match the rhetoric, *our words*, with the reality, *our behavior*. An example of trying to produce a successful match is represented by the condition of "color blindness." However, the frightening outcome of this condition is that because the nurse (provider) cannot see your color, she or he therefore treats you as if you are not a person of color—as if you are not who you are. With "color blindness," there's no attempt to work with your differences or acknowledge you, your family, and your heritage—your lived experience in this world. Color blindness is just one example; any difference the provider chooses not to see does not acknowledge you as a whole person.

Another interesting perspective to consider: Are nurses really angels of mercy with no hesitancy or bias in working with any patient? I suggest that we are human, and like others, we carry baggage gathered from our families and experiences throughout our lives. The work we do at times may be angelic work performed by nonangelic, rather human providers.

"Diversity is not solely dependent on one's ethnicity, race, or cultural background. Diversity is much more than the color of one's skin, but it is not color blind. Embracing diversity means a converging of all of the wonderful qualities that each of us brings to nursing. To exclude diversity is to rob nursing of a richness of the human being. Diversity is revealed through communication patterns, nursing activities, and the nurse-patient relationship. Diversity embraces differences and promotes an exchange of ideas and practices to enhance nursing. It is a worldview, not a point of view."

–Gina Diaz, DNP, MPH, APHN-BC
State-Licensed Health Officer

"Diversity is no longer theoretical. The concept now represents a few current realities. The first minority-majority generation is moving forward in our educational system. They are in middle school now. The majority white boomers are aging out of the workforce. Now what do we do?"

–Deborah Washington, PhD, RN
Director, Diversity,
Patient Care Services
Massachusetts General Hospital

So at this point, for the nursing profession to be successful going forward in the area of diversity—meaningful inclusion—I recommend:

1. Practice a conscious, reflective struggle with differences in you and your work. It is worthy of every nurse.

2. Know that differences are universal for humankind. One can find them even in one's own family system. Search out the differences in your own experience and reflect on their meaning to you personally and professionally as a nurse.

3. Affirm that the 3.4 million nurses are nonangelic—yet faced with the privilege and power of being a nurse, they are undaunted by the opportunity to make a difference in the lives of others and themselves.

While these recommendations are directed toward the individual, they can be integrated into the performance expectations that institutional systems have of their staff, faculty, employees, and leaders.

It is important to note here that there is no transformation without leadership and no leadership without desire and a dream of opportunities and possibilities. For nursing to be successful in realizing meaningful inclusion of others, the dream must be transformed into a shareable vision that others can touch, taste, and actualize. Like any other problem that needs to be solved, a strategic plan with purpose and powerful resources over a realistic time period, punctuated with periodic evaluation and overall passionate leadership, is required.

With the changing demographics of the nation, the need for problem solving will not diminish. As noted earlier by the NLN diversity definition, the issue is larger than ethnic and racial differences. Nurses are now facing up to the reality that we may be biased against our students, faculty, and staff with disabilities. The LGBTQ (lesbian, gay, bisexual, transgender, and queer) community is underreported in the nursing literature and not acknowledged in the nursing community. With a predominantly female profession, we may tend to show micro-inequities and micro-aggression toward men in nursing. Extending beyond men, micro-oppressive behavior is usually demonstrated in all types of biased situations so that one does not stray into visible macro, politically incorrect territory. I recommend the following:

1. A mission/vision statement: Highlight diversity and meaningful inclusion through language that points out that diversity by the numbers is insufficient. The addition of meaningful inclusion provides a context for embracing, elevating, and committing to the complexity that differences bring to any system. The NLN's mission statement—promoting excellence in nursing education to build a strong and diverse nursing workforce to advance the health of the nation and the global community—is reinforced by identifying diversity as one of the dynamic core values of the organization. The NLN's

Vision for Achieving Diversity and Meaningful Inclusion in Nursing Education (NLN, 2016) provides additional clarification and support of the organization's purposeful, conscious intent in relation to diversity.

2. Plan development: Contract with a reliable consultant who can safely uncover issues and help the organization develop a plan in concert with your Culture of Health.

3. Support system: Use internal and community committees chaired by high level leadership to navigate the initiative over a period of time (3 to 5 years). The consultant works with the committees. Provide positive rewards for both types of committees. The work should count for promotion and tenure in universities and promotion in other types of healthcare settings. Show clear appreciation for the Community Committee—for example, by bestowing an award. The status of the meeting place is an important element.

4. Budget: The budget is essential. The level of commitment can be evaluated by the existence of a budget with appropriate personnel resources.

5. Low-hanging fruit: Focus on the experience of those who are diverse within your system. What can be done to improve the experience of engagement and meaningful inclusion?

6. Long-term goals: Develop a pipeline of travel into your organization for

those coming from diverse backgrounds. The availability of internal and community mentors as built-in support systems is significant. Leadership opportunities should be available at various levels of the organization.

7. Evaluations: For each staff member's evaluation, identify the expectation for involvement in the plan and its outcome.

The NLN (n.d.) definition of the excellence core value is "co-creating and implementing transformative strategies with daring ingenuity" (para. 1). With excellence, we can transform the culture of diversity and meaningful inclusion in our country for the beloved people we serve.

References

National League for Nursing. (n.d.). Core values. Retrieved from http://www.nln.org/about/core-values

National League for Nursing. (2016, February). Achieving diversity and meaningful inclusion in nursing education. Retrieved from http://www.nln.org/docs/default-source/about/vision-statement-achieving-diversity.pdf?sfvrsn=2

Adriana Perez
Assistant Professor
University of Pennsylvania School of Nursing
Consultant, Diversity Steering Committee
Center to Champion Nursing in America

Progress and Challenges in Growing a Diverse Nursing Workforce

–*G. Adriana Perez, PhD, ANP-BC, FAAN*

When *The Power of Ten* was first published in 2011, promoting the diversity of the nursing workforce made the list of the 10 most important issues facing the profession, and it continues to rank high today. National nurse leaders with expertise on diversity issues described the significance of the problem in relation to the health of the U.S. population and factors that contribute to diversity. The nurse leaders outlined practical, bold solutions that encourage awareness and open, honest discussions that allow nurses to look inward at personal preferences and prejudices, mentorship, and engagement of diverse nurse leaders. The discussion also included the need to develop broad strategic partnerships, as well as policy initiatives that address funding, institutional infrastructure, and admissions criteria.

The outstanding progress that our profession has made in many areas, including promoting academic progression, increasing the number of nurses serving on boards, and achieving full scope of practice in many states, may be attributed to the recommendations and call for action from the Institute of Medicine (2011) report *The Future of Nursing: Leading Change, Advancing Health*. These achievements must be acknowledged and celebrated. However, to ultimately achieve

discussion point

"Women have decreased the gender gap in many other professions, but in nursing, there is a reverse gender gap, which is slowly narrowing as the number of men in nursing increases. If the gender gap disappears, would nursing experience a shift in the balance of power and influence in the workplace?"

–Reynaldo R. Rivera, DNP, RN, NEA-BC, FAAN
Director of Nursing Research and Innovation
New York-Presbyterian
Assistant Professor of Clinical Nursing
Columbia University School of Nursing

"The benefits of a diverse workforce in education and practice are widely recognized. Nursing's commitment to a diverse workforce has been forcefully and consistently strong. Yet change is slow, and there are no easy answers or quick fixes. Nursing's credibility in caring for vulnerable populations is dependent on our ability to create a diverse workforce—within our educational and practice institutions at all levels."

–*Antonia M. Villarruel, PhD, FAAN*
Professor and Margaret Bond Simon Dean of Nursing
University of Pennsylvania School of Nursing

the vision of "leading change, advancing health" for our nation, the continued challenges that persist in growing the diversity of the largest healthcare workforce—nurses—must be addressed with the same level of commitment, urgency, and political will. In fact, the Committee for Assessing Progress on Implementing the Recommendations of the Institute of Medicine report *The Future of Nursing: Leading Change, Advancing Health* (Altman, Butler, & Shern, 2016) recommended making diversity a priority in the nursing workforce.

The increasing growth of Latinos and other immigrant populations from around the globe continues to drive the changing demographics of the United States. In addition, the rate of uninsured has decreased to historically low levels due to the implementation of the Patient Protection and Affordable Care Act (Public Law 111-148), which has increased the number of young, ethnically diverse, newly insured who will need support and guidance as they navigate our healthcare system for the first time. As a result, growing a workforce that is diverse, bilingual, and multicultural will be even more critical in promoting a Culture of Health in the future. Strategies to recruit diverse nursing students—particularly at a younger age through science, technology, engineering, and mathematics (STEM) programs and scholarships, as well as promoting holistic admissions—show promising outcomes that should pay off in the next 5-plus years. However, how do we strengthen the retention of the diverse students and nurses we have now and successfully encourage them to pursue higher education through both DNP and PhD programs? And equally important, how do we accelerate the growth of diverse nurses who serve on boards and pursue leadership positions and those who represent the next generation of nurse scientists and faculty? All of these groups are needed now and can fulfill the role of mentors and role models for new students.

Looking back at the recommendations for diversity from *The Power of Ten*, I know from working with the Future of Nursing: Campaign for Action that many of these recommendations have been or will be implemented at the local level. However, the following challenges contribute to the slow advances:

1. There is limited current and published research to help guide nurse leaders on implementing programs that might work in their community.

2. Even in areas where evidence that supports a broad range of recommendations does exist, only a few organizations seem to be following them.

3. While various sources of funding exist to achieve these efforts, long-term sustainability is difficult due to limited resources.

4. There is varied consistency on the data that state Action Coalitions, affiliated with the Future of Nursing: Campaign for Action, use to track diversity goals. Some states prohibit the direct recruitment of ethnic minority students.

5. The lack of ethnic minority faculty at every level, including the number of those in leadership positions, means that institutions that promote diversity and inclusion might reflect this only in their written mission, not in their everyday culture.

discussion point

"There is increased recognition within nursing of the stress and negative health outcomes that lesbian, gay, bisexual, transgender, and queer (LGBTQ) patients experience. However, the same is not true about the experience of nurses who identify as LGBTQ. Many LGBTQ nurses have concerns about coming out at work; therefore, they may conceal being LGBTQ due to fear of being discriminated against by colleagues, supervisors, and even patients. Respect for diversity is an important principle of nursing practice. As nurses we strive to create open and accepting environments for our patients. But what about our fellow nurses?"

–Billy A. Caceres, MSN, RN-BC, AGPCNP-BC
PhD Candidate, NYU Rory Meyers
College of Nursing

Since 2009, the National League for Nursing has made available a Diversity Toolkit that outlines strategies and resources for administrators, faculty, and workforce, yet it is difficult to evaluate how many states or organizations are aware of the toolkit or are implementing the recommendations described.

Leading change is not easy, and we have learned that we cannot promote diversity alone. Unlike other top issues in nursing related to education or practice, holding individuals or groups accountable for achieving diversity goals can definitely benefit from incentives in the form of funding, reimbursement for significant and sustained performance measures, or perhaps even accreditation. First and foremost, as a profession, we must make diversity a priority. While the issue has once again made the top 10 list according to nurse leaders nationwide, perhaps this time we can build consensus that it is the No. 1 priority and establish measures for what success looks like across practice, education, and leadership.

References

Altman, S. H., Butler, A. S., & Shern, L. (Eds.). (2016). *Assessing progress on the Institute of Medicine report the future of nursing*. Washington, DC: National Academies Press.

Institute of Medicine. (2011). *The future of nursing: Leading change, advancing health*. Washington, DC: The National Academies Press.

National League for Nursing. (2009, September 15). Diversity toolkit. Retrieved from http://www.nln.org/docs/default-source/professional-development-programs/diversity_toolkit.pdf?sfvrsn=4

Patient Protection and Affordable Care Act. Public Law 111–148. (2010).

Priority #4: Interprofessional Collaboration

In this section:

- Interprofessional Collaboration That Works: HIV/AIDS Model of Care

- Interprofessional Collaboration

As the care coordinator, nurses tend toward a collaborative nature. However, more work is needed in this topic, particularly as care moves outside the traditional hospital setting and is focused more around prevention and care in the community. Interprofessional collaboration is more than just working among multiple disciplines to help a patient achieve healthcare goals. Nurses and all disciplines need to have a deep understanding of the others' roles, including scope of practice, so that the right intervention is provided by the right discipline at the right time. Nurses do not need to provide all care, and delegation is key as nurses coordinate patient care.

Consider the following questions as you explore the essays in this section:

1. How do we improve collaborative/interprofessional healthcare STEEEP (IOM dimensions of quality: safe, timely, efficient, effective, equitable, and patient-centered) analysis?

2. What would it look like if leaders from different disciplines came together to find common ground for policy development?

3. How do we prepare individuals to practice and contribute across settings and in teams, as well as build skills in understanding connections in systems of care?

4. How can we support more collegial and balanced interprofessional collaboration among the different disciplines, including nursing, medicine, pharmacy, social work, and more?

5. How can we improve the function in teams as we know them and as they are evolving?

Note: The terms *interprofessional* and *interdisciplinary* were used interchangeably by some of the essay authors. To avoid confusion, the editors elected to use the term *interprofessional*.

" Imagine flying a plane alone with no co-pilot, no control tower, and no navigation system. That's essentially what happens when a person tries to practice nursing without the appropriate interprofessional education or team in practice. It's obvious that the practice world is increasingly complex, and the myriad of disciplines that participate in care on any given day is really quite mind-boggling. When new nurses join the workforce without appropriate interprofessional education, there is undue waste of clinical time and negative sequelae for the people receiving care. When I recently asked the president of a major medical center what his biggest problem was, his answer was instantaneous: continuity of care. Nurses are the essential linchpin for continuity, and each of us needs to step up, stop waiting for permission, and insist on team-based care that is coordinated and patient-directed—and then lead in fostering an environment that would not even imagine practicing without an interprofessional team. Faculty who teach in silos simply fail to provide the contemporary education that's essential in today's healthcare environment. "

–Terry Fulmer, PhD, RN, FAAN
President, The John A. Hartford Foundation

Interprofessional Collaboration That Works: HIV/AIDS Model of Care

–Stephen Perez, MS, RN, ANP-BC, ACRN

Stephen Perez
*Doctoral Student
University of Pennsylvania
Robert Wood Johnson
Foundation Future of
Nursing Scholar*

When I entered the field of HIV nursing in the early 2000s, the epidemic looked different from what it was in the early days of the epidemic, and it has continued to change dramatically between then and now. As a nurse case manager and relatively new nurse, I was thrust into a world of care coordination for a group of patients whose problem lists were extensive. And while my clinical nursing skills and judgment would be exercised regularly, I did not feel especially prepared for my role as a nurse on the interprofessional care team. I had heard of interprofessional care in coursework but hadn't had many opportunities to see this in practice. Yet in the HIV/AIDS world, interprofessional care was a standard practice that was built on a foundation of experience and policy initiatives; I would need to get comfortable in my new role as a contributing member of the team.

As policy evolved and the first iterations of the Ryan White CARE legislation passed, funding was dedicated to designing community-based programs where people living with HIV could receive comprehensive care, treatment, and support for any complication that arose from their disease (Saag, 2009). Interprofessional care had already proved successful in the inpatient setting, where mortality rates were high and options were few, mandating that colleagues stop simply working

"We are learning the benefits and value of interprofessional care—where health professionals practice in teams and put patients and their families first—is making a big difference in multiple ways. Nurses are playing a big role, not only as members of teams but as leaders in multiple ways—better patient outcomes, improved patient satisfaction, higher engagement of families, health professionals who enjoy working together, and changing the culture of healthcare."

–Barbara F. Brandt, PhD
Director, National Center for
Interprofessional Practice and Education
Associate Vice President for Education
University of Minnesota Academic Health Center

alongside each other and start making decisions together. Those collaborative practices transitioned nicely into community programs. In fact, what would become evidence-based standards for interprofessional practice in HIV care is essentially what grew from the Ryan White CARE delivery system (Gallant et al., 2011). Soon patients in many metropolitan areas could visit their provider, see their mental health therapist, refill a prescription, and enroll in benefits all at one care center.

Working in Ryan White funded programs built on that model trained me well to maximize the effectiveness of interprofessional care as a tool for ensuring better patient outcomes. I learned to leverage this skill as a case manager, nurse practitioner, and quality improvement consultant, and I eventually went on to teach this type of collaboration in clinical settings all over the country.

When I began teaching and precepting nurse practitioner (NP) students, I felt it natural that they embrace this model of care in their training. I encouraged them to take the lead in physician consultation, actively participate in team case discussions, and assist with providing guidance to other team members. However, I learned later that this wasn't the norm in other clinical placements, even though this participation is crucial for developing skills and building confidence as a clinician leader. Students' participation at this level is a crucial component to their education, because interprofessional care is a difficult skill to "teach." The skills needed for collaboration are built on core knowledge and principles of patient care but can be as nuanced as the team itself. This type of care is a skill that must be fostered through experiential learning, much like critical thinking and judgment.

Our priority in nursing education from baccalaureate to advanced practice remains focused on developing the means necessary for building clinical knowledge and skills. The importance of these proficiencies is not trivial, but we should be asking ourselves: "Does our nursing educational paradigm promote ongoing experiences in interprofessional collaboration? Or is this a skill to be developed after licensure and practice?" Depending on those answers, the next question should be, "How do we ensure our nursing students obtain this experience so that when they graduate, interprofessional care is the expectation and not the exception?"

Answers to these questions may hasten the need to expand our paradigm of nursing and advanced practice education. We should be advocating for our nursing and advanced practice students to prioritize opportunities not only to observe, but also to engage in and contribute to interprofessional care. This may mean getting additional experiences in community settings or dedicating a larger portion of inpatient training to participating in interprofessional rounds or family meetings. If clinical placements don't facilitate interprofessional care, then we must consider how to build this into our simulation-based teaching strategies. On a macro level, our broader policy agenda should include continued funding to develop and evaluate pilot programs that train health professions students within a true interprofessional care model. Finally, we must support clinical care models that emphasize interprofessional care, not as innovation but as standard of care. Once these models take hold, placing students in these practice environments will be the norm and not just a privilege.

Models of care like those developed during the HIV/AIDS crisis prove that true interprofessional collaboration and shared decision-making are the keys to better patient outcomes. A new nurse or APRN should not worry about the utility of her or his role on the interprofessional care team. Let's allow the lessons of the past to carry us toward the future. Let's embrace the role of nurses and students in the interprofessional care framework as leaders, participants, and advocates. Interprofessional care empowers our patients and our colleagues; why not let it also empower us, as nurses?

References

Gallant, J. E., Adimora, A. A., Carmichael, J. K., Horberg, M., Kitahata, M., Quinlivan, E. B., … Williams, S. B. (2011). Essential components of effective HIV care: A policy paper of the HIV Medicine Association of the Infectious Diseases Society of America and the Ryan White Medical Providers Coalition. *Clinical Infectious Diseases, 53*(11), 1043–1050. doi: http://doi.org/10.1093/cid/cir689

Saag, M. S. (2009). Ryan White: An unintentional home builder. *The AIDS Reader*, 19, 166–168.

Interprofessional Collaboration

–Brenda Zierler, PhD, RN, FAAN

All nurses may not have a shared mental model of what constitutes successful interprofessional collaboration, but we do know that having a common goal sits at the center of any collaborative effort. Whether the context is research, education, practice, or policymaking, interprofessional collaboration can be described along a continuum from minimal levels of interaction to high levels of interaction and integration; however, both require competencies in teamwork, team communication, roles and responsibilities, and values and ethics of a team (Interprofessional Education Collaborative, 2011). These competencies cannot be learned in a classroom and require purposeful team training in practice, policy, and research environments.

Brenda Zierler
Professor, School of Nursing
University of Washington (UW)
Co-Director, UW Center for Health Sciences
Interprofessional Education
Director of Faculty Development, UW Medicine's
Institute for Simulation and
Interprofessional Studies

In the last 6 years, there have been an increasing number of reports, funding opportunities, publications, and accreditation requirements supporting and promoting interprofessional collaboration as an approach to address complex and multifaceted problems in health, healthcare, research, and policy. The current challenge for the profession of nursing is not whether we embrace interprofessional collaboration, but how to successfully operationalize the concept of interprofessional collaboration. We have spent too many years talking about being invited to the table and now need to move forward and implement collaborative practice with willing team members.

There is a growing literature in the science of team science or team-based research due to the fact that research teams across all fields are more productive and have a higher impact than individual investigators (Vogel et al., 2014). Research has also shown that team-based clinical care can improve patient and systems outcomes (Barceló et al., 2010; Janson et al., 2009; Strasser et al., 2008). Recently, *The New York Times* published an article on how Google has studied various team characteristics to determine how to build successful and productive teams. Their conclusion was that two particular traits, "conversational turn-taking" and "average social sensitivity," were predictors of effective teams. In other words, making sure that everyone has a voice and equal opportunities to talk and being sensitive or empathetic to other members on the team (how they feel, if they are feeling left out, etc.) are important characteristics (Duhigg, 2016).

One of the research gaps in assessing the science of team science has been the lack of attention paid to individual and institutional traits that influence team outcomes. This issue is the same for healthcare teams, where individual and institutional traits affect how well an interprofessional clinical team performs to improve health outcomes. Unfortunately, there continues to be a gap between the education systems and healthcare systems related to team-based competencies.

"With healthcare reform has come a heightened national focus on addressing the challenging social, environmental, and behavioral conditions that contribute to our health. Addressing the interplay of complex health issues—like chemical dependency, mental illness, and unmanaged hypertension and diabetes—with sociodemographic challenges of poverty, homelessness, and violence requires an interprofessional approach. Nurses are faced with both the demand and opportunity to work collaboratively across sectors and must reach outside of their immediate professional circles to draw from the expertise of social service, law enforcement, criminal justice, and health professionals in order to develop collective solutions to extremely challenging problems."

–Katharine Eilers, MPH, MSN, RN
Kitsap Public Health District

Education systems continue to use outdated models of training that focus on the technical knowledge and skills in both healthcare and research, not on the science of how different professionals within a team work together to produce better outcomes. We could learn a lot from the business world.

Clinical and research teams have antecedent conditions (personal factors such as awareness and implicit biases, physical environment, institutional policies, leadership styles of nurse managers and chief nursing officers) and intervening processes (interpersonal conflicts and communication strategies, team members' experiences working together, and collaborative behaviors) that affect the outcomes associated with their teamwork. The question for nursing is, do we emphasize and teach nursing students about the antecedent conditions and team processes that influence how a team functions? As a researcher, I would like the profession of nursing to utilize the science of team science and change the way we educate students and faculty.

Knowing that context is extremely important for successful teamwork, I reached out to several nursing colleagues who are currently engaged in interprofessional collaboration in education, research, and practice (faculty scholar in interprofessional education leading educational innovations for advanced practice students, lead researcher of three grants evaluating the effectiveness of team-training to improve collaborative practice, patient safety officer and TeamSTEPPS trainer for a health system, two nurse managers, and outpatient clinic nurse). Because they are immersed in interprofessional collaboration, I wanted to know their perspectives about what nursing would need to do to be successful with interprofessional collaboration in the future. All commented on individual and institutional traits that would need to change for nursing to be successful.

"Introduce required elements demonstrating interprofessional components into programs such as Magnet status, Beacon Awards, etc., versus completely nurse-centric as it is now."

"Allow and encourage frontline staff to have an integral part in the development of programs on how best to increase interprofessional collaboration. It cannot be a top-down initiative."

"Identify areas that have done well with interprofessional collaboration and learn from that."

"Teach nurses communication skills, humble inquiry, critical thinking skills, awareness of their own implicit biases, how to contribute to psychological safety in groups, and ability to use and understand data to make changes to practice and evaluate whether those changes are effective."

"Ensure that nurses have the time to participate and collaborate. We need to eliminate barriers to their participation in team-based care (e.g., time) and help them understand and value what they bring to the team—not just being present and listening but actively involved with a role that adds value to patient care."

"Establish a common language so that health professionals can communicate more effectively."

"Understand the need to be mutually respectful, willing to compromise, secure and confident in one's professional value to not be easily threatened, and willing to speak up and challenge others."

"Teach nurses how to stop unproductive conversations and inappropriate behaviors. If an MD is yelling at the front desk, my nurses would hide versus coming to the aid of the nurse involved and asking the person to stop or move the situation into a better place. Then they would talk about this person and how horrible he or she is instead of stopping the behaviors. Most of us would stop a peer or MD from doing something unsafe to a patient, so why do we not immediately assist when communication is inappropriate? Both have huge patient safety implications."

"Teach advanced practice nurses how to present cases and encourage public-speaking skills. Recently, several ARNPs turned down the opportunity to collaborate on an interprofessional team to provide didactic content and cases because they were not 'comfortable' presenting in front of physician colleagues."

"Willingly embrace new ways of doing things. The older generation needs to model this if the younger generation is to believe that interprofessional collaboration is important."

"Have morning briefs with patient care technicians, medical assistants, and nurses to develop a plan for the day. The physicians don't always show, but that doesn't stop us from collaborating and working together to improve care."

For nurses to be successful collaborators on interprofessional teams, we need to educate and train nurses in team science across the learning continuum (from prelicensure education to graduate practice to continuing professional development) and provide opportunities for them to practice these skills with other health professionals. However, we may need to get our own house in order first: Practice *interprofessional* collaboration; learn to collaborate with each other across education, practice, research, and policy; and close the gaps so that we have a shared mental model of the value of interprofessional collaboration. Then we can work together toward a common goal of preparing nurses for the future.

References

Barceló, A., Cafiero, E., de Boer, M., Mesa, A. E., Lopez, M. G., Jiménez, R. A., … Robles, S. (2010). Using collaborative learning to improve diabetes care and outcomes: The VIDA project. *Primary Care Diabetes, 4*(3), 145–153. http://doi.org/10.1016/j.pcd.2010.04.005

Duhigg, C. (2016, February). What Google learned from its quest to build the perfect team. *New York Times Sunday Magazine.* Retrieved from http://www.nytimes.com/2016/02/28/magazine/what-google-learned-from-its-quest-to-build-the-perfect-team.html?_r=0

Interprofessional Education Collaborative Expert Panel. (2011). Core competencies for interprofessional collaborative practice: Report of an expert panel. Washington, DC: Interprofessional Education Collaborative. Retrieved from http://www.aacn.nche.edu/education-resources/ipecreport.pdf

Janson, S. L., Cooke, M., McGrath, K. W., Kroon, L. A., Robinson, S., & Baron, R. B. (2009). Improving chronic care of type 2 diabetes using teams of interprofessional learners. *Academic Medicine: Journal of the Association of American Medical Colleges, 84*(11), 1540–1548. http://doi.org/10.1097/ACM.0b013e3181bb2845

Strasser, D. C., Falconer, J. A., Stevens, A. B., Uomoto, J. M., Herrin, J., Bowen, S. E., & Burridge, A. B. (2008). Team training and stroke rehabilitation outcomes: A cluster randomized trial. *Archives of Physical Medicine and Rehabilitation*, *89*(1), 10–15. http://doi.org/10.1016/j.apmr.2007.08.127

Vogel, A. L., Stipelman, B. A., Hall, K. L., Nebeling, L., Stokols, D., & Spruijt-Metz, D. (2014). Pioneering the transdisciplinary team science approach: Lessons learned from National Cancer Institute grantees. *Journal of Translational Medical Epidemiology*, *2*(2), 1027–1050.

"The evidence makes it clear: Interprofessional collaboration is a critical component of delivering safe, quality care. After years of talking about it, interprofessional collaboration should now be standard at all healthcare organizations, but it is not. Physicians, nurses, therapists, pharmacists, and other healthcare professionals should be learning together while still in school so that it feels natural, not forced, when they move to practice. On-site education provided at the workplace must also be interprofessional, not siloed. A well-functioning team should respect and learn from each other. Ultimately, it benefits consumers and the care they receive."

–Cheryl Hoying, PhD, RN, NEA-BC, FACHE, FAAN
Senior Vice President, Patient Services
Cincinnati Children's Medical Center

Priority #5: Systems Thinking

In this section:

- From No to Negotiation

- Reimagining Nursing's Contributions

"Nursing's voice should be loud and clear as U.S. healthcare transitions from an illness system to a health system. Nurses must know and practice with the entire system of care being the focal point for every 'user' of healthcare services. No longer can the focus be just the four walls of the hospital, but nurses must create a healthy and health-conscious culture for all, no matter where or when the 'user' enters the system of care!"

–Rhonda Anderson, DNSc(h), RN, FAAN, FACHE
Chief Executive Officer
Cardon Children's Medical Center

Systems thinking is a vital skill set for all nurses if nursing is to change healthcare as it should. Regardless of the systems in place, everything is interrelated. Understanding how this interrelationship works leads to sustainable, effective, and efficient outcomes. While reading the essays in this section, consider the following questions and issues:

1. A system has many parts, so what is your role in your current system at a local, state, and national (or even international) level?

2. With regard to payment models, how do we ensure that nurses are able to demonstrate their contributions to adding value in a cost-effective way?

3. How do we facilitate a basic understanding of systems and systems engineering—skills for both leadership and participation in evolving our health systems and improving health?

4. How do we change the economic model of healthcare in the United States?

5. How do we facilitate understanding The Big "P" Politics versus the small "p" politics of being in this world? This includes international work with international colleagues.

6. How do we teach and manage the politics of organizational systems—leadership, authority, power, and competition?

7. How can nurses actively engage in and lead the transition from a system for healthcare to a system for health?

From No to Negotiation

—Suzanne Miyamoto, PhD, RN, FAAN

NO. Two simple letters forming one word that can either stop or spur action. When it comes to the nursing profession, I have found that the word typically incites the latter—a call to action, an opportunity for education, a chance to reverse the tide. This reaction is very much the same in the world of policy and politics. In this complicated arena, the word "no," more often than not, translates to negotiation. In essence, this initial response is merely a launching pad for what will be the final product. Our history shows that both nurses and legislators are capable of seeing a way forward despite an initial negative reaction. Yet these two powerful engines for change often proceed down parallel tracks resisting collision, when it is essential that they come together and collaborate.

At the core of the profession is a nurse's professional responsibility to be a patient, family, and community advocate. Nurses champion the needs of those who are vulnerable, frightened, confused and, in many cases, have no voice at all. There is no hesitation or fear, only action. However, asking nurses to advocate at the national level on behalf of their profession, and in turn their patients, is often met with hesitation or trepidation, resulting in the word "no." So let's negotiate.

Suzanne Miyamoto
*Senior Director of Government Affairs
and Health Policy
American Association of Colleges of
Nursing (AACN)*

First, we need to start with why a nurse may say "no" to engaging in big "P" Politics. Members of Congress, lobbyists, and others engaged in politics fall on the bottom of the spectrum when it comes to the Gallup poll regarding honesty and ethical standards (Gallup, 2015). Nurses, on the other hand, have earned the top spot on this continuum for more than 10 years. Angels of Mercy (Kalisch, Begeny, & Newmann, 2007) meets *House of Cards* (Willimon, 2013). The two do not necessarily mix. I often have nurses tell me they cannot stand politics. Yet, politics is everywhere in our lives, our homes, our schools, and our workplaces— no one can hide from politics. As the old saying goes, "If you can't beat them, join them." Another reason could be explained by the seminal work of political scientist Mancur Olson (1965), whose theory of collective action introduced the notion of a "free rider." Essentially, in large groups, like registered nurses who number more than 3 million (National Council of State Boards of Nursing, 2016), it is harder to tell who is *not* doing the work when all are receiving the benefits secured by some. Another reason is education. Do nurses understand the implications of non-action, or worse, indifference?

It has been my experience that one of the largest challenges is education. You cannot change what you do not know. The American Association of Colleges of Nursing's *Essentials Series* includes, at all levels, curriculum on health policy and advocacy. The question remains, like any subject, how well is this information retained, but also taught? This query, among others related to educating a generation of nurses who have a basic grounding in policy and politics (the two can never be separated), is currently being grappled with by AACN's Faculty Policy Think Tank. At the same time, we know that nurses specialize, whether it be oncology, nephrology, or policy. Not every nurse has to be a policy nurse, but we do need more nurses with specialized knowledge in big P Politics.

This road is not easily traveled. One seeking to influence policy at the national level will hear "no" quite often. But remember, "no" leads to negotiation. Contemporary politics has manifested into something far beyond its original and natural intent—"the art or science concerned with guiding or influencing governmental policy" (Merriam-Webster, n.d.). Nurses learn the art and science of our profession, so we can also learn the art and science of politics. If there is one phrase to capture the profession's need to be politically active, it would be moral courage (Kidder, 2005). As the cover of Kidder's book so eloquently states, moral courage is "taking action when your values are put to the test." If your values do not align with modern day politics, consider the need for moral courage. Nurses must advocate for what is necessary to improve the state of health and healthcare nationally and globally. In the end, do not take *no* for an answer. Let "no" be the catalyst for change and the first step toward negotiation.

"Nurses caring for patients in any setting must have an appreciation of the systems of care and support available to the patient beyond that setting. Patients and families rely on nurses to explain, interpret, and navigate the complex healthcare system that is both foreign and frightening to them. Effective nursing care includes equipping the patient and family to continue the plan of care into the next setting. An understanding of the nested systems of family, community, and healthcare services is crucial to successful care transitions."

–Jane Englebright, PhD, RN, CENP, FAAN
Chief Nursing Executive and
Senior Vice President, HCA

"Many healthcare interventions and innovations that work under controlled conditions or temporarily do not have their intended effects on care improvement in real practice. System factors mediate everything and often not for the best. Systems thinking is essential to making real progress in improving safety and quality of care."

–*Linda H. Aiken, PhD, RN, FAAN, FRCN*
The Claire M. Fagin Leadership
Professor of Nursing
Professor of Sociology
Director, Center for Health Outcomes and
Policy Research
University of Pennsylvania

References

American Association of Colleges of Nursing. (n.d.). *Essentials series*. Retrieved from http://www.aacn.nche.edu/education-resources/essential-series

Gallup. (2015). *Honesty and ethics in professions.* Retrieved from http://www.gallup.com/poll/1654/Honesty-Ethics-Professions.aspx

Kalisch, B., Begeny, S., & Neumann, S. (2007). The image of the nurse on the internet. *Nursing Outlook, 55*(4), 182–188.

Kidder, R. M. (2005). *Moral courage.* New York, NY: Harper.

Merriam-Webster. (n.d.). Full definition of politics, 1b. Retrieved from http://www.merriam-webster.com/dictionary/politics

National Council of State Boards of Nursing. (2016, January 23). Active RN licenses: A profile of nursing licensure in the U.S. Retrieved from https://www.ncsbn.org/6161.htm

Olson, M. (1965). *The logic of collective action: Public goods and the theory of groups.* Cambridge, MA: Harvard University Press.

Willimon, B. (Writer), & Foley, J. (Director). (2013). *House of cards.* Los Gatos, CA: Netflix.

Reimagining Nursing's Contributions

–*Mary D. Naylor, PhD, RN, FAAN*

What is the basis for systems thinking? Systems thinking has been proven effective in addressing a range of complex issues, typically involving a number of players within and across organizations, by enabling them to see the "big picture." Systems comprise multiple interconnected parts, including people, processes, and data. High performing systems also recognize that they are affected by—indeed are often dependent upon—larger systems. For example, primary care practices or hospitals are part of the U.S. healthcare system, which, in turn, is a component of America's larger society. Optimizing the entire system's performance is the primary goal and the basis for defining success.

Why is systems thinking so important to health outcomes? Major changes in the U.S. healthcare system, stimulated by the Affordable Care Act, have placed a spotlight on the critical role of systems thinking. Traditionally, the United States has described the core output of health systems as care that is accessible, person-centered, equitable, timely, efficient, and effective. An abundance of evidence suggests that the emphasis on these outputs has substantially improved medical care but not the health of our society.

Mary D. Naylor
*Marian S. Ware Professor in Gerontology
Director, NewCourtland Center for Transitions and Health
University of Pennsylvania School of Nursing*

"Nurses embrace treating a person as a whole being, not just the disease that impairs good health. Consequently, when providing care, nurses consider the person's relationship with his or her family, loved ones, community, and environment, as well as the person's ability to perform social and professional roles and other factors. Similarly, nurses should consider how the services they provide relate to the healthcare system—the efficiency and coordination of the care delivery system; the perspective of payers who finance care delivery; the type, amount, quality, and cost of services that they are providing; and whether the services are provided to all people. Not paying attention to these components of the healthcare system is akin to failing to pay attention to the person as a whole and only focusing on the disease."

–Peter Buerhaus, PhD, RN, FAAN
Professor of Nursing
Director, Center for Interdisciplinary Health Workforce Studies
College of Nursing
Montana State University

The desired output of any system is largely driven by the values of its leaders. Systems thinking enables leaders to reframe their goals and responses to increasingly complex health issues. Health rather than healthcare, quality of life rather than quality of care, and dying with dignity rather than death are then recognized as the "big picture" challenges. The powerful opportunity offered by a systems orientation is unleashing healthcare professionals' unique contributions in addressing the needs and preferences of individuals and populations, while wisely choosing how to use finite resources.

What are key opportunities and challenges for nursing in advancing a systems approach to healthcare? A distinguishing contribution of nurse-led research is the identification of outcomes that matter to people. In contrast to the dominant medical model focused on diseases, for example, nurse scholars have emphasized a holistic model to comprehensively address health challenges. Nurse-led interventions target individuals and their family caregivers and communities, are multidimensional in nature, and focus on longer-term outcomes. Healthcare's shift toward accountable care systems, population health, and value align exceedingly well with the knowledge generated by nurse researchers. A key opportunity is for all nurses to accelerate local health systems' use of such solutions. While fostering adoption or adaptation of evidence-based strategies represents an important first step, optimizing a health system's performance will require investment in the creation and management of a learning health system.

More than any other discipline, nurses understand how the healthcare system's capacity to meet people's needs is dependent upon larger social and economic forces. Yet, our profession operates in a system that has narrowly defined its boundaries. For example, a prevailing view has been that healthcare clinicians or organizations should not be held accountable for the social determinants of health. The most vulnerable people in our society, those who depend on us the most, often are challenged by poverty, low literacy, behavioral issues, and other social challenges. While the healthcare system is not responsible for all social problems, nurses and all health professionals are accountable for doing all that they can to mitigate the negative impact of these issues on people's health and quality of life. A key opportunity is for nurses to maximize their knowledge and skills in capitalizing on partnerships with other sectors of society to address the complex needs of all members of society.

One example of an evidence-based, systems-oriented approach to addressing healthcare priorities is the Transitional Care Model (TCM). The TCM is an advanced practice nurse-led, team-based care management strategy designed to improve the care and outcomes of at-risk, chronically ill older adults with complex health and social needs. This model also targets family caregivers, aptly described as the "invisible workforce." In multiple National Institutes of Health-sponsored clinical trials and foundation-funded translational studies, the TCM has consistently demonstrated improved patient health and quality of life outcomes as well as healthcare savings. Currently, this proven care model is the basis for initiatives spearheaded by many local communities to move to a higher value health system. To a large extent, the success of this model is its emphasis on the "big picture"—both the human and societal consequences of chronic illness and the recognition of the need for robust partnerships that extend well beyond traditional healthcare to assure longer-term positive outcomes for vulnerable patient populations.

Unfortunately, systems thinking does not come naturally. Similar to other health professionals, nurses have been socialized to focus on personal versus systems responsibilities for outcomes. In no way does this latter perspective offer an opportunity to "blame the system." If anything, a systems orientation strengthens expectations regarding individual performance. Rather than assuming sole responsibility for outcomes for a select group of people, all now share accountability for the performance of the entire team. This mindset presents nurses with a huge opportunity to expand their roles and contributions. At the same time, nurses will be challenged to restructure their relationships with other health team members and, most especially, the people they support.

Call to Action. The following suggested strategies are proposed to enable nurses at different stages of their careers to maximize on the possibilities offered by systems thinking:

1. Apply systems thinking in identifying and designing solutions to major challenges.

2. Co-create systems with patients, families, communities, healthcare team members, and other stakeholders.

3. Participate in the selection of more meaningful system "outputs" (i.e., measures that matter).

4. Promote a health system that is continually learning.

5. Seek leadership opportunities related to system redesign.

6. Encourage systems to embrace new partnerships.

7. Advocate for healthcare delivery practices and policies (including payment) that extend beyond traditional boundaries, and recognize and reward accountable health systems.

8. Participate in changing an organization's culture to emphasize teams and the performance of the entire system.

Conclusion. This essay attempts to characterize the complexity of healthcare redesign and the promise of a new pathway to achieve what matters most to people using systems thinking. A systems orientation presents all healthcare professionals, and especially nurses, with a unique opportunity to align professional and organizational responsibilities in the work of articulating, advocating for, and putting into practice models of healthcare delivery that more closely align with the goals and needs of our society.

"Health transformations occurring now and in the coming years must be based in systems thinking approaches. Nurse leaders are the ones to make their voices be heard for these transformations. They have seen how the unjust economics created by our decades-old, perversely incented structures have amplified an unevenly functioning sick system. Just as nurses know whole person care, executive nurses must build in whole systems thinking in whole service delivery and payment reforms to build up a true system of health and well-being. Strategic innovations in population health, high level communications of nursing key value proposition, disciplined data collection by nursing researchers, and nurses' ability to drive a new client engagement will accelerate the successes of health transformations. Courageous nurses need to take bold, calculated, and supported risks to drive faster change at all levels. Colorado's investments in transforming Medicaid into an accountable care-coordinated framework have yielded major financial savings, happier providers, and better health outcomes for our 1.3 million clients. Onward!"

–Susan E. Birch, MBA, BSN, RN
Executive Director
Department of Health Care Policy & Financing
State of Colorado

Priority #6: Voice of Nursing

In this section:

- Sage Leader
- Voice of Global Nursing
- The Voice of Advocacy

"Nursing is the most respected profession. As such, nursing's voice must be heard through our leaders. Nurses need to be at the public policymaking tables. If not, we are 'on the menu.' We are the diamonds in the rough of the healthcare system, and now is the time for us to share our glitter and lead with our voices."

–Bethany Hall-Long, PhD, RN, FAAN
Delaware State Senator

The *voice of nursing* must be spoken in a cohesive manner, regardless of the country in which a nurse practices. The profession of nursing has deep international roots and a rich international history. It was important to get that perspective in this section, which contains a national (United States) and international perspective; both apply to anywhere a nurse practices. With nursing ranked consistently as the most trusted profession in the U.S., it is important that the profession continues to use the voice of nursing to advocate for the health and wellness of all people.

In this section, consider the following issues and questions as you read the essays from our contributors. What can you add? How can you contribute to the voice of nursing, regardless of where you live?

1. How do we get nurses to take advantage of opportunities beyond nursing that position them to make a big impact?

2. Advocacy/political voice: We all have a voice; how do we use it to make healthcare better—political action committees, boards, political office?

3. How do we continue to develop nurses' abilities to communicate in strong, powerful ways with deliberate messaging and seize opportunities as they arise?

4. How do we establish a cohesive voice and support our nurse colleagues around the world, given the diversity of educational preparation, practice levels, and settings globally?

5. How do we get the voice of nursing at every table where health and health-care are being discussed and ensure it is seen as a "valued" voice, and not a "token" voice?

6. How should nurses prepare themselves to serve on committees and boards?

7. How do we get all nurses to engage in and use the political process and the public at large to address health issues?

Linda Burnes Bolton
System Chief Nurse Executive, Vice President of Nursing, Chief Nursing Officer, and Director of Nursing Research Cedars-Sinai Medical Center Principal Investigator Cedars-Sinai Burns & Allen Research Institute

Sage Leader

–Linda Burnes Bolton, DrPH, RN, FAAN

Leadership is a practiced life art that is honed by personal and professional experiences. Throughout my life as a woman, an African American, a nurse, and a leader, I've had many opportunities to gain experiential knowledge from being present in multiple settings. I've learned to value the wisdom of others as I journeyed along the pathway to being of use in society. I've listened intently to my inner voice cautioning me not to take myself so seriously and to hold fast to a dream of an equitable, inclusive, and caring world where all can thrive.

The poet Maya Angelou is one person whose wisdom has guided me. Her poems, such as "Still I Rise," have inspired and lifted me up when I found myself at a turning point in my life. Spending a week on the farm of child-rights-activist Marion Wright Edelman surrounded by leaders in education, social service, health, art, science, music, film, drama, and politics was a turning point early in my career. The experience affirmed that my commitment to valuing and caring for humans by seeking to remove the barriers to productive, healthy lives was the right path for me. The collective wisdom of the gathering helped me to visualize the possibility of a just world, if each of us is willing to commit to doing the work to make that vision a reality.

Throughout my professional career, I have promoted the importance of knowledge acquisition and application of best person-centered practices in the provision of health services. The quest for knowing, as poet Langston Hughes professed to be of importance in "Hold Fast to Your Dreams," propelled me to begin a lifelong journey seeking to help others to have and realize dreams of health, security, and prosperity. I've always used my knowledge, skill, and will to engage others from diverse backgrounds. My mother, who inspired me to seek to help humankind in anyway I can, at all times, has been and remains my rock.

Mentors have provided guidance and started me on a journey of servant leadership. It began with working with my peers and family living in poverty. One can choose to become jaded when impoverished, or one can choose to address the situation by identifying what is needed to rectify the problem. Education was the pathway out of poverty for me. Education led to acquisition of knowledge and skills and prepared me to advance in my chosen profession and society. The pursuit of knowledge on what could be done to have a better life prepared me to become a nurse and to follow my true north star—excellence in human caring for all people with respect for who they are as fellow human beings.

"It is my belief that there is no situation in work or life that has to be accepted as "this is as good as it gets." A common characteristic of leaders I admire is that they see the world through a lens of what is possible, and then find a way to make it happen. When facing both opportunities and challenges, nurse leaders are in an ideal position to create conditions for success by bringing about the best possible outcomes for everyone involved. Rather than sitting on the sidelines, it is both a privilege and a responsibility for nurse leaders to emerge and raise their voices now! With the complex health issues facing populations across our country at stake, we are compelled to step up, take action, and model the way. It is incumbent upon us to fulfill the trust that is placed in us by making leadership decisions every day in big and small ways to bring about better health for individuals, families, and communities. Our greatest leadership legacy will be evidenced by the health and quality of life of those we are privileged to serve."

–Laurie Benson
Executive Director
Nurses on Boards Coalition

Following my true north, I pursued education on what could be done to close the gaps in living conditions. Why, I asked at the ripe old age of 12, did so many of my classmates in junior high school leave before completing their education? Why did so many have only one parent living at home? Why did so many African American, Hispanic, and Native American girls and boys fail to finish high school? Why were so many poor children having children before turning 16 or finishing high school? Why did so many people in poverty die so young, especially African American males? I kept questioning, just as Florence Nightingale did: Why was all the premature death that was occurring in my neighborhood, city, state, and nation necessary? I began my quest to help others obtain education as a pathway out of poverty: to call the circle of engaging others on the journey to create an inclusive society where all have access to fair housing, living wages, clean air and water, and the opportunity to a better life. Nursing has been that pathway for me and others. My lifelong journey of being of service to others provided me with opportunities to influence individuals, social and health professionals, educators, policymakers, and foundations. I have been a circle caller all of my professional life and have found active engagement of diverse voices to be an effective process for improving the human condition and society.

Calling the Circle

I was first introduced to circle calling through participation in a leadership program sponsored by the American Organization of Nurse Executives. The art of engaging others and creating space where conversation can occur freely is a valuable skill that I have used throughout my career. Whenever there is an opportunity to gather others to seek their perspectives—to answer questions about the design, delivery, and evaluation of health and social services—leaders must call the circle. I have called the circle to address the elimination of health disparities, working with health professionals, politicians, housing authorities, food banks, charitable foundations, and consumers. My network of humans willing to participate in the challenging work of human caring is quite large. Each individual brings integrity to the table and her or his willingness to inspire others. Sage leaders have learned over time and life experiences the value of being inclusive.

Reflecting on Self and the Ability to Influence

Looking back on my 46 years in nursing has caused me to pause and reflect on the choices I have made. The decision to pursue graduate education early and to acquire knowledge from urban planning, sociology, health policy, and public health put me on the path to servant leadership. I have learned the value of followership. Paraphrasing from Aristotle, great leaders are first great followers, and he who has never learned to follow can never command. Wise leaders continually seek to understand before seeking to be understood and listen first before speaking or acting. Listening and understanding are two vital leadership behaviors. A third is being selective when asked to join a collaboration, organization, or professional society. Ask yourself: Will my participation facilitate my ability to influence larger society? Choosing to accept positions and appointments with governing bodies; professional societies; and education, health, and social policy organizations has allowed me to influence a great many people and institutions.

My commitment to human caring has been the north star that has guided my career and contributions to achieve a just, healthy, and inclusive society. It is important that we refuse to accept lives that are impaired and lost. Each of you must stand up and call the circle, practice inclusiveness, and remain committed to upholding the value of nursing. We must work together for everyone to have access to safe, quality healthcare.

If the doors to quality healthcare can't be opened, knock the doors down! Stand up and lead colleagues!

References:

Angelou, Maya. (1978). *And still I rise.* New York, NY: Random House.

Baldwin, C. (1997). *Calling the circle, the first and future culture.* New York, NY: Bantam.

Hughes, Langston. (1932). *The dream keeper and other poems.* New York, NY: Alfred A. Knopf.

Frances Hughes
Chief Executive Officer
International Council
of Nurses

Voice of Global Nursing

–Frances Hughes, DNurs, RN, Col (ret), JP, ONZM

In an era of globalization and health system reform, many developing and industrialized countries are reforming their healthcare systems to best use the limited resources available to improve the health status of populations. Now, more than ever, the nursing profession must draw on its expert knowledge and experience to improve healthcare by helping shape effective health policy.

Effective advocacy requires health professionals to take the initiative. For many nurses, this may mean moving out of their comfort zone to learn new leadership skills and take advantage of opportunities to influence policy or people outside of nursing. To do this, it is essential that nurses first clearly understand how policy is made and implemented and its wider context. Without this understanding of policy development, nursing will not be included in the process. Therefore, nurses need to have a good knowledge of the broader environment that impacts on health and of the relevant key players and networks. It is essential we keep abreast of developments in the local community, nationally, and internationally. It is also essential that nurses learn who the key players are, such as politicians and government officials.

Once the right people have been identified, the right message needs to be delivered. This requires good communication and interpersonal skills, and the International Council of Nurses (ICN) has three leadership programs that provide the training needed for this.

Influencing the design and implementation of policy in health and in other related areas to achieve better health outcomes is one of ICN's priorities. We lobby governments to include nurses in their delegations to the World Health Assembly and, as a nongovernmental organization (NGO) with official relations with the World Health Organization (WHO), we are able to bring our own delegation and make interventions on behalf of the nursing profession. We also work with United Nations agencies, supporting and impacting the Sustainable Development Goals and the new Global Strategy on Human Resources for Health.

It is our duty as nurses to ensure that our voice is heard and valued, not only for the profession but also for our patients. Health professionals who support the principles of participation and empowerment should seek to encourage patients to undertake advocacy themselves and become agents of change in their own areas of concern. Public perceptions of the validity and legitimacy of a campaign are enhanced if those most directly affected by the problem or issue are seen to be actively involved.

"Nurses are often leaders in the shadows. We are most comfortable working behind the scenes to lead change. Some do this well, but when there is a critical mass of shadow leadership, nursing's power and potential are overlooked by others. We must come out of the shadows!"

–Diana J. Mason, PhD, RN, FAAN

Successful advocacy requires gathering evidence in the form of scientific issue-related knowledge. Advocacy based on inaccurate information or false claims is unethical, potentially injurious to public health, and a wasted effort. Nursing associations should be seen as expert resources on important healthcare issues. One way this can be accomplished is through the development of clear policy positions that are supported by data from relevant publications, research studies, and respected opinions. In addition, well-researched and well-placed articles can help influence opinion.

Forming strategic alliances with other organizations can add weight to your opinions and broaden your audience. Where important policy issues are involved, unity within the nursing profession is essential. If legislators and policymakers perceive divisions in the nursing community, they are unlikely to listen to a nursing "voice" that does not reflect some unity within the profession. To be truly effective, these alliances should go beyond the profession. One example is the World Health Professions Alliance (WHPA), of which ICN is a founding member. The WHPA brings together global organizations representing the world's dentists, nurses, pharmacists, physical therapists, and physicians. It works to improve global health and quality of patient care and facilitates collaboration among health professions and major stakeholders.

In conclusion, leadership at the policy level means that nurses can influence decisions on health programs and services and can have a voice in setting the health agenda, determining priorities for resource allocation, and designing health programs and services. Nurses need strong political commitment, political skills to influence decisions, dedication of resources, a healthcare system that can deliver care to those who need it, and skillful application of sound knowledge and ethical principles in our nursing practice.

Jesse Kennedy
Staff Nurse, Intensive Care Unit
PeaceHealth Sacred Heart Medical Center
Director at Large, Recent Graduate
American Nurses Association
Board of Directors

The Voice of Advocacy

– Jesse M. L. Kennedy, BSN, RN

Nursing has a unique voice in the world. Nurses come from all walks of life, with many joining the profession as a second or third career—which offers a great array of backgrounds that inform that voice. The diversity of specialties within nursing offers the ability for nurses to develop specialized and unique skills that provide unique insight into the profession. The amazing array of foci within the nursing profession also allows nurses to have long and varied careers that bring a great diversity of generational viewpoints. Nursing has been ranked the most trusted profession for the last 14 years, according to Gallup's annual polling—which adds a great weight and duty to utilize this voice for the health of our patients and the health of our profession.

If we are to fully utilize the great solutions and ideas that come from this wide array of perspectives, we have to ensure that nurses know the value of their voice and that part of their role as a nurse is to use their voice to advocate in many forms. Using nursing's voice is central to our role as nurses. According to our profession's cornerstone documents in the American Nursing Association (ANA) Nursing Code of Ethics, "The nurse promotes, advocates for, and protects the rights, health, and safety of the patient" (American Nurses Association, 2015, p. 9). The mandate to advocate is central.

With 3.1 million nurses (Kaiser Family Foundation, 2016) in the United States alone, nursing should be leading the way in policy development and guiding healthcare into the next evolution of healthcare delivery. However, not enough nurses join their voices to the broader discussion. The biggest issue facing nursing's voice is participation, rather than the understanding that it is necessary. We need participation at the bedside, in the boardroom, and in the halls of legislature to truly utilize that voice.

If participation in the broader healthcare discussion ranges from innovation and policy development on a facility level all the way to vocal advocacy in the national legislative agenda, we must broaden the definition of advocacy in nursing. Nurses are comfortable with bedside advocacy; it is what we do every single day for our patients and their families. The change in thinking has to come in extending that same passion and advocacy to other patients who may encounter the same issue and advocating for policy change at ascending levels. Chances are that issues each nurse encounters have happened somewhere before and will happen again, and it is imperative to develop a sense of advocacy that sees this connection to the broader populace. When we see that connection, it becomes second nature to protect and advocate beyond the bedside. Seeing the need for your advocacy beyond an individual experience is the first big change that is needed.

"Nurses are the keepers of patients' stories. As such, they have a unique perspective on healthcare systems and a singular opportunity to champion effective change. By working to take the "what if," "why not," and "should be" from the bedside to the broader organizational and policy levels, nurses can drive transformations in effective care delivery. They can open the door to innovation that heals our patients and advances health and well-being across our communities. It is the power behind the voice of nursing."

–*Angela Patterson*
DNP, FNP-BC, NEA-BC
Chief Nurse Practitioner Officer
CVS MinuteClinic

Nurses are becoming more comfortable with the idea of advocacy in the board-room, especially with the larger focus nationally to get more nurses on boards. These national efforts include the Nurses on Boards Coalition, with a goal of getting 10,000 nurses on boards by 2020, and the Future of Nursing: Campaign for Action. Many facilities now have collaborative governance structure to provide the best possible view to inform decisions on the facility level. Despite our numbers and authority as direct-care healthcare providers, nurses often lack the experience needed to navigate the boardroom effectively. While there are several resources now available from ANA and many other national nursing organizations, competing interests for nurses' time and the sheer amount of time spent on boards cumulatively leave nurses behind the curve in many boardrooms. The second change needed to strengthen nursing's voice is to ensure that development of the skill set needed in the boardroom becomes a core aspect of nursing education and continuing education.

Nurses thrive in the team setting and are core to care coordination, which offers a great skill set for ensuring that a policy or law continues to fruition and has the maximum benefit for our populace. Nurses possess the bedside expertise, epidemiological knowledge, and problem-solving skills that legislators and local officials need to make informed decisions. Advocating in the halls of legislature is not much different from what nurses do every day, but it requires some additional experience and training to truly be effective. There needs to be an active initiative to equip our nurses with the opportunities needed to advocate for policy as well as the tutelage needed to fully engage their voice in policymaking.

Engaging nurses and advancing these advocacy goals are no small tasks. Because nurses come from so many walks of life and span multiple generations, nursing leaders must make a concerted effort to engage broadly and in ways that work. Each generation prefers communication in a different way, which requires that nursing reach out every way possible, from printed communication to interactive applications and everything in between. Technology has provided us with countless ways to interact with nurses; the key will be to ascertain which platforms and formats provide relevant information quickly to nurses when they need them the most. Nursing can utilize the teamwork and engagement skills that we utilize every day in team-based healthcare by working with technology companies and content providers to discover unique ways of communicating and empowering nurses to use their voice.

Finally, with the ever-approaching, widely assumed retirement of great numbers of baby boomers and experienced leaders, we have to ensure that a huge wealth of knowledge is not lost. Younger nurses are excited and eager to engage their voices if given the opportunity. We will be doing a great disservice to the future of nursing if we cannot provide skilled mentorship and tutelage to nurses interested in honing their leadership skills. Nursing needs an intentional effort to continue training and building new leaders to ensure they can bear the mantle that has made nursing the indispensable and innovative profession that it is today. We all know that we stand on the shoulders of nursing giants; let's make sure that we are empowering the next generation of leaders to continue the legacy!

Two actions that must be taken:

1. Work with intention to foster leadership growth and transition for the next generation of leaders.

3. Work with leaders of other industries, especially tech fields, to develop responsive and intuitive information-delivery methods that engage and inform when nurses need them most on one level and offer in-depth studying when time permits.

References

American Nurses Association. (2015). *Code of ethics for nurses with interpretive statements*. Silver Spring, MD: Nursebooks.org

Kaiser Family Foundation (2016, January). Total number of professional nurses. Retrieved from http://kff.org/other/state-indicator/total-registered-nurses/

"I have considered leadership over the years and know that my style was heavily influenced (or affirmed) by the sociologist Leonard Cottrell. Cottrell was one of my thesis advisors. I would not call him a mentor. He did not take me on with a view of long-term guidance of my career. But he and his ideas were as helpful as any I have ever come across. Cottrell taught me the most useful phrase in leadership: the concept of interpersonal competence. Briefly, it is that skill or set of abilities that allows an individual to shape the responses he or she elicits from others. Correctly predicting the impacts of one's own actions on another person's definition of a situation, having a varied and large repertoire of possible lines of action, and using the necessary interpersonal resources to employ appropriate tactics are components of interpersonal competence. That concept has informed individual and group contacts I have had, and when I forget it, I am miserable."

–Claire M. Fagin, PhD, RN, FAAN
Dean Emerita, Professor Emerita
University of Pennsylvania Interim President, 1993-94

Priority #7: Global Stewardship

In this section:

- Nurses United in Global Stewardship

- Global Stewardship

Nurses take care of the health of people, regardless of where they live. Being a global steward means that nurses are part of the solution to issues that impact health in a range of topics. In this section, essay contributors focus on the global perspective. With increased travel, rise of global developing markets, and the internet—to name a few—we are increasingly becoming a global society where what impacts one part of the world will affect everyone, regardless of distance. The Ebola and Zika viruses have shown us the speed and reach of healthcare crises for all people.

As you read this section, consider what you can do to be a global steward from wherever you are.

1. How do we commit to public health, environment, and climate change, all multidimensional global challenges for healthcare providers, scientists, lawmakers, and regulators?

2. How do we review health and environment platforms of candidates during election cycles?

3. How do we advance health for the global community?

4. What can we do regarding the global impact of emerging diseases? Consider Ebola at the height of the crisis. Who is in charge of this?

5. With an increased number of poor working environments and a large retiring nursing workforce, what have we learned from international recruitment so that one country doesn't destroy the healthcare infrastructure of another?

"Whether it is leading chronic disease management programs, nurse-led services, creating new models of care, or building a bridge for peace, nurses are stepping in and up to the global challenge to provide universal access to care."

–Anne Marie Rafferty, CBE,
DPhil (Oxon), FRCN, FAAN
Professor of Nursing Policy
King's College London

Elizabeth Holguin
Doctoral Student
University of New Mexico
Robert Wood Johnson Foundation Nursing
and Health Policy Collaborative Fellow
Jonas Nurse Leader Scholar

Nurses United in Global Stewardship

–Elizabeth Holguin, MPH, MSN, FNP-BC

What is global stewardship exactly? The term suggests social responsibility and social justice, awareness of the natural environment surrounding us, interpersonal and intercultural understanding, and empathy for human suffering. The nursing profession embodies these qualities wholeheartedly.

Tasked with implementing an infection control program in a small government hospital in Sierra Leone, I proudly arrived "well-prepared" with all of my resources, plans, and academic preparation. Obviously, I was going to ensure that everyone wore gloves properly, cleaned equipment with the proper bleach solution, avoided cross-contamination, and followed correct handwashing techniques. My first goal was to observe the nurses and their work on the wards as well as in the operating room. My well-intentioned plans soon disintegrated before my eyes.

Malaria is extremely common in Sierra Leone. I saw that almost all the window screens had large holes in them. That's okay, I thought; we have mosquito nets. Well, these too had large holes, putting all patients at further risk of illness. The patients were lying on straw-filled mattresses; some were fortunate enough to have a sheet or blanket. Chickens, dogs, and cats ran freely through the hospital—these were certainly not part of my plan for aseptic dressing changes and wound care. I

'It is a big world. It has been said that the world has become smaller because we are more connected by better transportation, communication, and digitalization. But, nurses dedicated to reaching patients and communities in the remote corners of the globe still experience a world that is big and full of health risks and challenges with limited human resources. The world is big for the 20 million nurses who have worked and continue to work, while devalued and undercompensated, to develop innovative strategies to deliver care and make a difference in people's lives. Nurses have always been at the center of global healthcare as they use their knowledge to provide evidence-based care, their passion to promote health and well-being, and their compassion to care for vulnerable and underserved populations, increasing access to care, decreasing suffering, and alleviating pain. The world will truly become small when 7 billion people are assured access to universal healthcare and when there are no health disparities within countries and between countries. It will become a small world when every member of the healthcare team is valued and equitably compensated—and when all team members are able to use their full knowledge and expertise to achieve global health goals. Until then, the world will remain very big. **"**

–*Afaf I. Meleis, PhD, DrPS(hon), FAAN*
Professor of Nursing and Sociology and Dean Emeritus
University of Pennsylvania School of Nursing

did not have to concern myself with proper glove-wearing or handwashing techniques. There were no gloves unless an individual nurse had enough extra money to purchase them and bring them to work. There was a sliver of soap remaining with which to wash their hands.

In the operating room, I could not monitor sterile technique because I could barely see. The electricity flickered on and off unreliably that day, as it always does. Two women arrived that day from their villages for emergency caesarian sections because their labor did not progress as expected. Because of inadequate prenatal care and little to no health education, coupled with unreliable transport, they made it to the hospital too late. They lay on cold metal stretchers in a dark hallway awaiting their turn to have their lifeless, grey babies pulled from their wombs. I watched, grey in color myself, as the nurses tried their best to revive the infants with a mouth-operated suction device—no electricity, so no power suction. Their efforts were useless.

In the tuberculosis ward, I noticed only women. Where are the men, I wondered? I was taken to a barn-like structure where men infected with tuberculosis were lying on pieces of cardboard in 110° heat because, according to the administrator, the men and women needed to be separated. I convinced the staff to hang a sheet dividing the ward and carried the men, too weak to stand, to their beds.

Families camped outside the hospital for days, cooking to ensure that their admitted family members had meals and running to the pharmacy to buy the medicine that was prescribed. If they lacked funds to buy the medication, the patients did without.

Scarce resources left nothing dedicated for nursing education. Nurses were often volunteers with little to no training. Through no fault of their own, they performed care improperly and hung intravenous without a thought to what had been hung previously—any bag would do.

No patient advocacy could take place since nurses could not even advocate for themselves. Recently, thousands of nurses sacrificed their lives to care for Ebola-stricken patients. Was the number of nursing deaths due to the virulence of the disease? Possibly, yet what would the outcome have been with proper infrastructure, dedicated health spending, and adequate equipment and education?

Would we stand for these conditions here? Absolutely not. Yet, our fellow nurses work this way each and every day. Nurses in the United States are looked upon as innovators and visionaries. Can we venture beyond the bedside and classrooms and forge a path to the policy table?

Decisions are constantly made on our behalf and for our patients, often without our voice represented. Let us lead the way for nurses around the world and exemplify how becoming involved in public policy, health policy, public health, or economics will inform our practice and the way in which we care for patients. The solution to health lies in the minds of the largest healthcare workforce in the world.

What is global stewardship? Social responsibility and social justice, awareness of the natural environment surrounding us, interpersonal and intercultural understanding, and empathy for human suffering. Let us unite as a profession and put our wisdom, empathy, and unique perspective to good use to impact fellow nurses in our global community and the patients they strive to care for every day.

Global Stewardship

—Judith Shamian, PhD, RN, DSci (Hon), LLD (Hon), FAAN

Every time I think we have exhausted the insights and lessons learned from Florence Nightingale, I discover a new thought, writing, or idea that renews my realization about what an amazing woman and icon she was. We in nursing are blessed to receive guidance from such great leaders who shaped the path for us. At the same time, I so often reflect on how our present would be different if we had continued to walk in the paths that our ancestors paved for us.

Judith Shamian
President
International Council of Nurses
President Emeritus, Immediate Past
President, and CEO
Victorian Order of Nurses

As the 27th International Council of Nurses president and as an individual concerned with local, national, and global public policy—including, but not specifically, health policy—I wish we had taken the policy "yellow brick road" and had continued in the path that Florence Nightingale walked. Many books have been written about her work, but one of the documents I cherish—and I have the original in my possession—is the *Report on the Site of the Royal Victoria Hospital, Presented to the House of Commons by Command of Her Majesty* (1858). In this 190-page document, which has amazing witnesses examining everything from the soil on which the building is built to the air quality, is "Miss Nightingale's evidence" on page 26. There, she talks about ideal bed numbers in a unit, necessity of light, ventilation (natural and artificial) and warming, comparative cost assessment, kitchen requirements, and more.

"Across the globe, the performance of the healthcare system depends upon the quality and education of those who give care—nurses."

–*Franklin A. Shaffer, EdD, RN, FAAN, FFNMRCSI*
Chief Executive Officer
CGFNS International

The reason for this lengthy comment on this report is to remind us that nursing has at its roots not only aspects of care, but also aspects of systems management health policy at the highest level. Stewardship (n.d.) is defined by Dictionary.com as "the responsible overseeing and protection of something considered worth caring for and preserving." As nurses and global citizens both at the individual and the communal level, we need to ask ourselves, "What is our stewardship, and how should we exercise it in this global complex world?"

Today when we examine the Sustainable Development Goals (SDGs), many of the goals are areas that nurses care deeply about. The SDGs are relevant to all countries—developed, developing, middle, and low income countries. As nurses we need to advocate and be stewards of this global crucial agenda. Whether we talk about health, poverty, hunger, or environmental health, we know these are all essential elements of healthy and productive families and communities. As nurses we are committed to health far beyond illness. As nurses we care for our immediate environment, our communities, and our families, but we need to engage in a much broader agenda that goes beyond our immediate environments.

For some reason, too few nurses engage with global issues and agendas. My biggest concern is that I seldom encounter nurses or nursing organizations that have input into these global public policy agendas. These agendas have significant impact on the lives of the 7 billion people on earth and on the well-being of the planet in the coming years.

Over the last 60-plus years, nursing has surged forward as a great science-based profession with an extensive body of knowledge, but at the same time, our influence in managing healthcare, systems, and public policy is limited. Why is that? There are many theories and ideas, and we all have our opinions, but the reality is that nurses in service are kept overly busy dealing with the day-to-day issues and in many ways are not "allowed" or "encouraged" to speak up on system issues—which are seen as the responsibility of the boards and presidents of these big institutions. On the other hand, academics have the freedom to speak up but they are swamped with research, publications, and teaching responsibilities. Far too often, the many great research results find their way to peer-reviewed publications, but do not find their way to the desk of decision makers, including politicians. I have been privileged to see national nursing organizations and academic centers like the WHO Collaborating Centers engaged in advocacy, research, and stewardship of global issues with sister organizations or countries that can benefit from the support that comes from these national associations and organizations.

As the nursing community, we have to ask ourselves a crucial question: "Do we have a moral, ethical, and professional responsibility to engage in global stewardship?

It is clear to me that the answer is a resounding *yes*!

"Unless we are making progress in our nursing every year, every month, every week, take my word for it, we are going back."

–*Florence Nightingale*

"It's hard to imagine nursing not having a global perspective. Clearly, human suffering and human caring know no borders. Nor do our origins and the wealth of knowledge we have to share with one another. Let us never forget that nursing in the US is but a branch of a tree planted by Florence Nightingale and others on another continent over a century ago. The shade it casts on human suffering is greatest when all branches flourish and join together in the work of caring."

–*Marla E. Salmon, ScD, RN, FAAN*
Professor of Nursing and Global Health University of
Washington

If the answer is yes, that we do need to be engaged in global stewardship, how are we going to make it happen? Truth be told, we need to turn the tide and make nurses active in public policy as quickly as we can.

As I look at my lifelong journey, my engagement in change started at the unit and hospital level by wanting to add value, make a difference, and have an impact on my immediate reality. This helped me to learn some of the skills required to propose and bring about change; this was a stepping-stone to advance my education, knowledge, experience, expertise, and also my confidence in taking on larger and larger issues and having a stronger and stronger voice and impact in influencing global health and well-being.

We have the knowledge, the evidence, the smarts, and the passion to change the course and seize our right to have a voice in global stewardship.

In addition to the clarity of the need for the paradigm shift, we need courageous men and women (nurses) who are willing to step up to the challenge and take on both elected and staff positions in key local, national, and global organizations like the UN agencies, European Union structures, political positions, and much more.

If we are real in our commitment to global stewardship, we have to act and act now.

References

Report on the site of the Royal Victoria Hospital, presented to the House of Commons by command of her majesty. (1858). London, UK: Harrison and Sons.

Stewardship. (n.d.). In Dictionary.com. Retrieved from http://www.dictionary.com/browse/stewardship?s=t

"A powerful nursing contribution toward universal access to health is the implementation of advanced practice nurses (APNs) around the world to increase the quantity and quality of primary healthcare providers in remote areas. Universal health coverage can shift from dream to reality through a shared vision, understanding unique cultural contexts, and a strong strategy to increase access to health in the first level of care. A global perspective on nursing is necessary to connect countries across the globe toward the advancement of universal health coverage."

–Silvia Cassiani, PhD, RN
Regional Advisor on Nursing and Allied Health Personnel
Health Systems and Services-Human Resources for Health
Pan American Health Organization (PAHO/WHO)

Priority #8: Practice Authority

In this section:

- Preserving and Emboldening the Advanced Practice Registered Nursing Role

- Practice Authority for APRNs

The first things many nurses envision when discussing practice authority are the barriers surrounding advanced practice registered nurses (APRN). However, practice authority must cover all levels of nursing practice, from RN to APRN. Many healthcare institutions facilitate less than full authority for RNs through policy and procedural practices they create. Full understanding of the legal scope of practice for nurses by every nurse is the first step to ensuring full practice authority. Additionally, we must work to continue to remove the legal and financial barriers for APRNs via legislation, but also the barriers to practice within hospitals, including medical staff privileges.

Consider these questions in regard to modernizing state-level scope of practice laws. How can you have a positive impact on these, regardless of your role?

1. How do we finish removing barriers for full practice authority issues and reimbursement of APRNs?

2. How do we provide clarity on APRNs' scope and a workforce plan to determine how many APRNs in each role and specialty are needed?

3. What are the facilitators that would allow BSN nurses to practice to the top of their education and training?

4. How can we achieve seamless portability of APRN license across state lines?

5. What laws need to be changed so that telehealth is an effective tool for RNs and APRNs?

"In an era of rapid change, raised public expectations, and ever-increasing complexity of health and well-being needs of society, it is essential for nurses to practice to the top of their education and training. This must become the norm for optimum clinical outcomes to be achieved and efficient, effective, and equitably distributed care is to be delivered to all citizens. Nursing is taking bold steps to protect the patient through maintaining state-based licensure whilst simultaneously, via our use of compacts, facilitating nurse mobility and modern approaches to high quality care delivery. Out-of-date legislation or archaic views toward the delineation of care have no place in a modern health system that needs to be evidence-based and team-delivered. With the increase in non-communicable disease, the crisis in prescription drug abuse, and the pending threat of globally transmissible diseases, any attempt to place restrictions on the capability and capacity of nursing's contribution to the health and well-being of society is a misplaced and misguided threat to achieving the triple aim."

–David Benton, PhD, RGN, FRCN, FAAN, NCSBN
Chief Executive Officer
National Council of State Boards of Nursing

Garrett Chan
Director of Advanced Practice
Stanford Health Care
Clinical Associate Professor
Stanford University School of
Medicine

Preserving and Emboldening the Advanced Practice Registered Nursing Role

–Garrett K. Chan, PhD, APRN, FAEN, FPCN, FNAP, FAAN

Healthcare reform is appropriately focused on increasing access to primary care to improve the disease prevention and health promotion of Americans to stay as healthy as possible for as long as possible. To meet those healthcare needs, advanced practice registered nurses (APRNs) are educated as generalists in one population focus: neonatal, pediatric, family/across the lifespan, adult/gerontology, gender-related, and psychiatric/mental health (NCSBN, 2008). Even as we transition from an illness and disease focus toward the new paradigm of health and wellness, a continuing need exists to manage chronic illness at both generalist and specialist levels.

Nurse practitioners (NPs) provide care along the wellness-illness continuum that includes health promotion, disease prevention, health education, and counseling, as well as diagnosis and management of acute and chronic diseases (NCSBN, 2008). Clinical nurse specialists (CNSs) manage the care of complex and vulnerable populations, educate and support interprofessional staff, and facilitate change and innovation within healthcare systems (Lewandowski & Adamle, 2009).

Many similarities exist between NPs and CNSs. Both acquire advanced clinical knowledge and skills that prepare them to provide direct care to patients and demonstrate a greater depth and breadth of knowledge, greater synthesis of data, increased complexity of skills and interventions, and great role autonomy (NCBSN, 2008). NPs and CNSs are also educationally prepared to assume responsibility and accountability to diagnose and manage patient problems that may include prescribing pharmacologic and nonpharmacologic interventions (NCSBN, 2008).

The two roles are also different in some ways. One difference is that NPs are educationally prepared as generalists who have a broad knowledge base across many illness states and body systems, while CNSs have in-depth education in a specialty area in a particular focus of practice beyond the population focus (e.g., cardiology, oncology, wound/ostomy care). Another difference is that the NP role has a much broader legal scope of practice in most states that allows NPs to have full practice authority as delineated by the National Council of State Boards of Nursing (2008).

The doctor of nursing practice (DNP) is an educational degree that has gained momentum as a practice-focused doctorate. The educational degree is distinctly different from advanced practice roles in nursing such as the CNS, NP, or nurse executive. There are eight DNP Essentials: scientific underpinnings for practice;

"We're going to need every nurse we can find, among legions of new, richly skilled, well-educated nurses, to provide the primary and preventive care, chronic care management, and care coordination that are going to be the core of a smooth-functioning, cost-effective, equitable healthcare system. AARP has been a long-time advocate for expanding the role of nurses to be allowed to contribute to the full extent of their capabilities. We want to help ensure that everyone in America has access to a highly skilled nurse, when and where they need one."

–JoAnn Jenkins
Chief Executive Officer, AARP

organizational and systems leadership for quality improvement and systems thinking; clinical scholarship and analytical methods for evidence-based practice; information systems/technology and patient care technology; healthcare policy for advocacy in healthcare; interprofessional collaboration for improving patient and population health outcomes; clinical prevention and population health for improving the nation's health; and advanced nursing practice (AACN, 2006).

Increasingly, many educational APRN programs are moving to the DNP as the conferred degree. When the DNP and CNS core competencies are compared, a surprising amount of overlap exists between the educational degree and the role. Therefore, NPs who are educated in DNP programs appear to be educated in CNS competencies. The only difference, then, for NPs seems to be the lack of advanced practice specialty content that is present in CNS education. To preserve the specialty education to meet the healthcare needs of Americans as complex and vulnerable populations continue to need care, we need to preserve the role and educational focus of the CNS in advanced practice nursing. While we can continue to prepare prelicensure CNSs to meet those needs, transition-to-practice programs for NPs can also fulfill the educational requirements to become a specialist APRN, also known as a CNS.

We are witnessing an increasing interest of NPs to gain specialty education and training as evidenced by a proliferation of postgraduate transition-to-practice programs such as APRN fellowships. To be clear, ARPNs are educated in their prelicensure master's or doctoral programs to meet core competencies to practice safely and at a high-quality level to meet the societal need for competent practitioners. Recognition that the need for CNSs and NP/CNSs is the emerging trend in advanced practice nursing will allow nursing to preserve the much-needed role of the specialist APRN—providing pathways for licensure, accreditation, education, and certification to assure the public that a fully educated specialist APRN is meeting complex health needs.

References

American Association of Colleges of Nursing (AACN). (2006, October). The essentials of doctoral education for advanced nursing practice. Retrieved from http://www.aacn.nche.edu/publications/position/DNPEssentials.pdf

Lewandowski, W., & Adamle, K. (2009). Substantive areas of clinical nurse specialist practice. A comprehensive review of the literature. *Clinical Nurse Specialist, 23*(2), 73–90.

National Council of State Boards of Nursing (NCSBN). (2008, July 7). Consensus model for APRN regulation: Licensure, accreditation, certification, and education. Retrieved from https://www.ncsbn.org/Consensus_Model_for_APRN_Regulation_July_2008.pdf

"It's a travesty that highly educated health professionals with rigorous training could be regulated to such a degree that they are actually prohibited from using their skills and knowledge. Such is the case with scope of practice constraints on APRNs. What other profession is so constrained? While opponents of full practice hide behind claims that independent practice is actually harmful to patients, this has never been proven. This line of thinking continues to sway elected officials to over-regulate nursing practice. Nurses must do two things: become much more actively engaged in the legislative process and widely disseminate the data that supports independent practice as a safe, cost-effective model of care."

–Laure Marino, DNP-EL, FNP-BC, GNP-BC
Director of The Primary Care Center @ Process Strategies
Charleston, West Virginia

Practice Authority for APRNs

–Margaret Flinter, APRN, PhD, C-FNP, FAAN, FAANP

Margaret Flinter
*Senior Vice President and Clinical Director
Community Health Center Inc.
Board Certified Family Nurse Practitioner*

It is remarkable to look back for a moment and see how far we have come in the steady march to full scope of practice authority for APRNs in the United States. Perhaps it's an example of an old saying, *what doesn't kill you, makes you stronger!* Every inch of progress for advanced practice nurses in earning the right to take full and transparent accountability and authority for their own practice has been hard-fought and won. The battles have played out on many levels, primarily in the state legislatures, where generations of state representatives have been listening, year after year, to testimony for and against revising state practice acts to allow for broadened scope of practice and, ultimately, full practice authority for advanced practice registered nurses (APRNs).

I'm a veteran of the decades of that steady march, with a particular focus on nurse practitioners. When I became a nurse practitioner (NP) in 1980, still in the early wave of the NP role and movement, I quickly realized what it meant to be invisible in a way I had never experienced. While the work was incredibly satisfying, that invisibility—using prescriptions presigned by my physician practice partner, ordering diagnostics in someone else's name—heightened my sensitivity to what marginalized people experience. When I hear the oft-quoted but always powerful words of Martin Luther King Jr. that "The arc of history is long but it bends towards justice," I am reminded of the historical struggle against culture, tradition, attitude, and regulatory constraints that once limited the full expression of our work and ability to contribute.

We arrive at this exciting moment in time with an estimated 260,000 APRNs in the United States (National Council of State Boards of Nursing, 2008). In 21 states and the District of Columbia, APRNs enjoy full independent practice authority. Well-organized, relentless campaigns continue in the other states, focused on achieving the regulatory changes recommended in the APRN Consensus Model developed in 2008 by the National Council of State Boards of Nursing.

In my home state of Connecticut, now considered a full independent practice state for NPs, that independence comes only after 3 years and 2,000 hours of practice as an APRN, a compromise that allowed the legislation to move forward. We practice against a backdrop of all of the well-known challenges: workforce shortages; an explosion of known chronic illness and new public health threats; and advances in science, technology, and practice transformation that give us unprecedented tools to meet those challenges. I firmly believe it's no longer a matter of if, but when, all states will move into the category of full practice authority states for APRNs, and we will be that much closer to ending the shortages of primary care providers for all—but particularly for our underserved populations.

In my own community health center organization, NPs now outnumber physicians almost two to one. They practice independently and as part of fully integrated teams in primary care centers and school-based health centers. NPs hold leadership positions as medical directors and key committee chairs, and they function as principal investigators conducting research through our Weitzman Institute. They precept legions of students and residents and serve as faculty for our national Project ECHO programs, training primary care providers across the country in the most complex problems seen in primary care. Most of them came "of age" as NPs long after the early battles for recognition, and it is a joy to see them assume and own their professional independence, autonomy, and recognition with ease and grace. This is the way it should be for successive generations.

As APRNs, we have taken it into our own hands to ensure that we are always evolving as science and practice change. The creation of the DNP as a terminal practice degree and the development of postgraduate residency and fellowship programs speak to that continual development. These innovations were not externally mandated, legislated, or tied to practice authority, but both respond to the needs of our next generations of APRNs and advance our capacity to fully deliver on the promise of the highest quality care.

Beyond the care of individuals, whatever the setting, we have earned the responsibility to be leaders and agents of change in advancing a Culture of Health in our

"When every state grants statutory authority upon APRNs, conferring the freedom to practice to the full educational extent, our population will realize the value and worth of their services. Should this conference be accompanied by a paradigm shift to a Culture of Health, the United States could receive an A rating for its accessibility, acceptability, availability, accountability (quality), affordability, and affability in healthcare."

–Loretta C. Ford, EdD, RN, PNP, FAAN, FAANP
Cofounder, Nurse Practitioner
Dean and Professor Emerita, University of Rochester
School of Nursing

communities, states, nation, and world. The patient before us is our concern—but so are the whole population, community, and larger society. Scope of practice acts neither restrict nor ensure our seat at the tables of influence and decision making in business, government, healthcare, and civic society. Indeed, we have legions of RNs and APRNs in powerful roles in these arenas—but we need more.

Let me share one powerful example of why we need APRNs to have both full practice authority and full representation at the tables of decision making. As I worked on the first draft of this essay a few months ago, I wrote, "People are literally dying in the streets by opioid overdose. A huge need exists for medication-assisted treatment of opioid addiction. But the Drug Addiction Treatment Act of 2000 restricted prescribing buprenorphine, an often lifesaving drug for opioid addicts, to physicians, regardless of state prescriptive authority for APRNs." I noted that this single decision had profound consequences, drastically limiting access to this medication-assisted treatment for opiod addiction for years, even as the demand for such treatment exploded. Fast-forward several months, and I am pleased to report that through the concerted efforts of many stakeholders, President Obama signed into law the Comprehensive Addiction and Recovery Act of 2016 (CARA) on 22 July 2016. Among its many provisions, it allows NPs and PAs to prescribe certain medications for treating opioid addition. This is further evidence of recognition of the vital role we play in meeting the nation's healthcare needs, and of the steady march of progress.

Full practice authority is a base and bedrock on which to advance change. It will support, but not in and of itself create, the future that we want to see: a future in which all nurses, both RNs and APRNs, can make their greatest contributions to health and healthcare. Our success will be based not just in thinking about our practice as APRNs, but in realizing how we can support other members of the healthcare team in making their greatest contributions. One needs only to look at the emerging role of RNs in primary care to see that the core competencies of RN practice—patient education, clinical assessment, care coordination, and treatment both independently and under standing orders—have the potential to be a "force multiplier" in increasing the size and capacity of our primary care providers through the use of a team-based model of care, all within the RN scope of practice. And in turn, we expect that our RNs will support and mentor medical assistants, health coaches, lay workers, and even family caregivers who, in turn, can expertly manage important elements of care.

Full practice authority makes visible, but not inevitable, our force as a profession that is empowered, but not isolated, in our quest to deliver on the promise of healthcare as a right, not a privilege.

Reference

National Council of State Boards of Nursing. (2008, July 7). Consensus model of APRN regulation, licensure, certification, and education. Retrieved from https://ncsbn.org/736.htm

"There is only one provider group in the world that can solve our global health challenges: nurses! There is no one more caring or honest with health consumers than a nurse. And it is that connection that motivates health consumers to pursue better health for themselves. Yet, with all the positive impact nurses have locally and globally, we take them for granted, and we put them through the ringer politically in the United States and globally by controlling their ability to practice to their fullest extent of their license and education. My plea to all is to once and for all unleash the power of nursing ... when we do, the world will change for the better!"

–Tine Hansen-Turton, MGA, JD, FCPP, FAAN
CEO, National Nurse-Led Care Consortium

Priority #9: Delivery of Care

In this section:

- The Changing Face of Care Delivery

- Delivery of Care: The Who, What, and Where

Delivery of care is a very complex topic. The nursing profession has a rich history and deep roots within community and public health. With healthcare reform, we are moving from an acute care-centric delivery system to one that focuses on prevention and the care continuum. As the largest profession of healthcare providers, nursing must be at the table to influence, develop, implement, and evaluate care delivery models.

In this section, our essay authors were asked to address issues and questions about delivery of care from their perspectives. Consider the following questions and issues as you read the essays:

1. How do we reevaluate and rethink the models we now use and redesign delivery settings (RN role; interprofessional teams; patient, family, and community engagement)?

2. How do we develop the business case and dissemination plan for innovative models?

3. As we shift from acute-care to community-based and preventive care, this includes changing nurses' roles and preparing them for these "new"roles. Who is responsible for this?

4. How do we collectively support nursing leaders to step up (with other professionals) to solve the issues for which we should be "primary"—primary care, palliative care, end-of-life care, care transitions, long-term care, midwifery, anesthesia, and community health centers?

" Study after study, decade after decade, evidence has mounted on the impact of nurses' practice environments on everything from nurse satisfaction to the quality of patient outcomes. It's not surprising that a practice environment that enables the most robust contribution of the unique knowledge, wisdom, and expertise of registered nurses results in improved patient outcomes. Yet, so often, when people are discussing strategies for achieving the triple aim—improving the experience of care, improving the health of populations, and reducing per capita costs of healthcare—they fail to understand, address, or improve the quality of nurses' practice environments. Autonomous authority of nursing practice, participation in professional governance, and support for high quality and safety are all necessary to elicit the best in nursing practice. Locally, nationally, and internationally, nurses must influence and create the social, political, professional, and economic factors that ensure their practice environment elicits and enables the best in the nursing care they have to offer. "

–Marla J. Weston, PhD, RN, FAAN
Chief Executive Officer
American Nurses Association

5. How do we create a process to retool the workforce to assume a larger role in primary health education, prevention, and coaching beyond the APRN role?

While there are best practices and models that have explored and even locally solved these issues, are they scalable? We need to be active participants in order to change the delivery of care.

The Changing Face of Care Delivery

–*Kathleen D. Sanford, DBA, RN, FACHE, FAAN*

Kathleen Sanford
*Senior Vice President and Chief Nursing Officer
Catholic Health Initiatives (CHI)*

Since the inception of the Patient Protection and Affordable Care Act in 2010, hospitals and systems have strategized and planned for what some have dubbed the "next era of healthcare." Nursing leaders have been involved in the envisioning and implementation of both business and clinical changes that must accompany this new age. Of course, we've also concentrated our thinking and efforts on how our profession will best serve individuals and communities in both the near future and the decades to follow. This is not a new issue for nursing. Our history is replete with historical changes in our practice models, practice locations, and even how we educate and prepare ourselves and our colleagues in response to an evolving world. What *is* new is the pace at which everything around us is transforming.

Ready or not, our environment is altering faster than most of us perceive. Driverless cars that cannot crash into each other will soon be a reality that radically changes trauma and emergency care. Genome therapy holds the promise of not only curing disease but also preventing it. Inventions such as IBM's Watson, constantly updated with medical research results and textbook knowledge, combined with a person's blood and urine lab work, will probably be better at diagnosing all diseases better (and faster) than a team of expert clinicians. A cellphone application already exists that can compare a self-taken photo of a person's skin to a data bank full of photos of diagnosed rashes or lesions and advise on whether a mole is worthy of further medical intervention. At the 2008 American Organization of Nurse Executives (AONE) annual meeting, futurist and inventor Ray Kurzweil informed the audience that research currently progressing in this country will mean that health problems as diverse as diabetes and obesity will be a thing of the past in our lifetime. We cheered these prognostications, even as some of us felt frissons of incredulity and others wondered what these predictions will mean for our profession.

The former (slightly skeptical) group might need to be reminded that Kurzweil awed and amazed us by appearing at our conference as a hologram. (A health problem kept him from coming in person.) It was the first time most (if not all) of us had taken part in real-time, "face-to-face" virtual interactions. Today, just 8 years later, we think nothing of participating in virtual meetings, whether they occur in conference rooms or from our own desktop computers. Kurzweil's message, which echoed Richard Buckminster Fuller's 1981 depiction of the pace of human accumulation of information, was a reminder that all human knowledge is doubling at an accelerating rate. So, while our profession has done an admirable job of changing to meet healthcare needs in the past, the transformational needs of this next era will be our most challenging because we will need to change ourselves and our models of care delivery much more rapidly.

What will it mean to nursing if there is less trauma as well as eradication of much disease in the next 2 decades, if not sooner? Some say we will largely move from caring mostly for the sick to helping people stay well, something nurses have always advocated. To that, I say, "Yes, *and* ..." The "and" is a caution that we must understand that our part in wellness will eventually have to be rethought, too. Helping people manage chronic conditions won't be a big role if chronic conditions such as diabetes are no longer an issue for large numbers of the population. Teaching people about diet and exercise (almost always the cornerstones of what we need to teach today for wellness) may become much less important when people have applications on their phones or wristwatches that tell them what to eat or when to exercise.

While none of us has a crystal ball, we can be assured that our work will not look the same in 2025. Thought leaders for this profession need to be thinking at least 10 years ahead so that we can prepare for a future that is radically altered. We need to observe and project changes that will call for different nursing care. For example, imagine some of the societal changes coming soon: In a world where trucks, cabs, and delivery vehicles don't require a driver, how many people will lose their driving jobs? (Hint: recent news reports state that driving is the number one job category for American men.) When grocery stores adopt technology beyond the self-service kiosks of today to the touted future where a shopper just

"As we continue to shift our focus from volume to value, nurses are ideal members of the healthcare team to lead initiatives and move us toward a Culture of Health. When nurses are viewed as an expense to organizations, shortcuts are taken that restrict nurses' abilities to provide the highest level of care. We need to design and support practice environments that empower nurses to practice to the full extent of their education and training. Key stakeholders must view nurses as value-added members of the healthcare system who, when allowed to utilize their knowledge and skill set fully, are capable of transforming how healthcare is delivered."

–Dan Lose, DNP, RN
University of Iowa Hospitals & Clinics

rolls his or her cart past a "beam" by the door and is automatically charged appropriately for everything in the cart, what will happen to the grocery workers? What about other retail businesses, when goods are ordered online and delivered by mechanical drones? If you believe, as I do, that humans want a purpose (and that work *is* a major purpose), when much of the work we do evaporates, will we face a crisis in mental health brought on by depression and lack of purposefulness? Even if you are an optimist who is certain that new jobs will be created by our rapidly escalating technology, will we not face the same mental health crisis when individuals are not prepared for these new jobs? What if not enough work exists for all? Will we be called upon to help people find meaning and joy in increased leisure time?

You may think this issue (or similar societal challenges we are about to experience) is for sociologists, psychologists, or social workers to deal with, rather than nurses. I disagree because the very essence of our holistic profession is to promote health (mental, physical, spiritual) for individuals and populations, and that means for actual or potential health problems. To prepare ourselves for future care delivery, we must consider what the realities of both will be and take steps to be ready to deliver what people need. Nurses are about human touch and contact, which will always be needed. We also must help our current and future nurses understand and accept that rapid change will be their constant reality, and they will need to be prepared to repeatedly transform themselves and their work.

In the near future, (the next few years), we will be considered successful if we develop evidence-based nursing care models that embrace use of technology; influence healthcare decision makers to try innovative models based on carefully constructed business cases; design new nursing roles moving away from acute care to community-based and preventive care; support our nursing leaders as they make the cost and quality case for nurses serving as primary clinicians in areas we have historically embraced (palliative care, end-of-life care, community health, wellness care, etc.); and create processes to retool the nursing workforce to take a larger role in primary care. In the longer term, our success should be judged not by what we do to preserve current practices or elevate our profession, but by what we do to support and build the health of individuals, communities, and the world. That is, after all, the true definition of *care* delivery.

Reference

Buckminster Fuller, R. (1981). *Critical path*. New York, New York: St. Martin's Press.

"To the uninitiated, all hospitals must seem more or less the same in terms of nurses' work environments. But the opposite is true. I know from personal experience that one hospital floor can be toxic from nurse bullying, while its sister unit across the hall is a haven of collegiality. Units can be well-organized and designed for efficiency, or they can require hundreds of extra nurse steps just to get the day's work done. Better work environments equal better nursing—a common sense formulation that, unfortunately, few hospital administrators understand."

–*Theresa Brown, PhD(h), BSN, RN*
Hospice Nurse and author of The Shift

Delivery of Care: The Who, What, and Where

–Andrea Tanner, MSN, RN, NCSN

When Miss Colorado, Kelley Johnson, performed a soliloquy at the 2015 Miss America Competition, she shared with the world her story of delivering nursing care. Afterward, a nationally syndicated television show host commented on Johnson wearing a "doctor's stethoscope." The ensuing commentary revealed that the general population does not understand delivery of care or the role of nurses in care delivery. Those within the healthcare system also struggle with how to best deliver care using nurses, physicians, and other healthcare practitioners. The United States spends more than any other country on healthcare while coming in last of all developed countries in preventable death rankings and 43rd in life expectancy (Nolte & McKee, 2011; World Health Organization, 2013). The nation is left asking who should deliver care, what healthcare should look like, and where such care should occur for better outcomes.

New models of care delivery look beyond physician-led care and consider the unique role that nurses can play beyond the bedside. An American Nurses Association (ANA) news brief written after passage of the Affordable Care Act detailed promising new delivery of care models with a recurring theme—returning to healthcare that promotes the essence of nursing with holistic, coordinated,

Andrea Tanner
*School Nurse and Coordinator of Health Services
New Albany-Floyd County Schools
Indiana
National Association of School Nurses (NASN)
Epinephrine Resource School Nurse
National Certified School Nurse*

wellness-focused care that addresses the patient, family, and community (ANA, 2010). The Robert Wood Johnson Foundation funded a search for delivery of care models and found that 23 of the 24 most promising models "elevated" the role of nurse from simply caregiver to "integrator" of care (Joynt & Kimball, 2008). A program report and highlights from exemplary care models can be found at www.rwjf.org. When nurses are at the helm of chronic care case management and multidisciplinary care coordination, our nation's healthcare system sees financial savings, decreased infections, improved nurse and patient satisfaction rates, improved communication between disciplines, increased follow-up psychiatric care, and increased quality time spent with the patient (Brooks, 2014; Lee et al., 2014).

With an opportunity for nurses to play a greater role in delivery of care and improved outcomes, the range of care nurses can provide is far-reaching. The very definition of nursing details the profession's ability to handle the "alleviation of suffering through the diagnosis and treatment of human response, and advocacy in the care of individuals, families, communities, and populations" (ANA, 2016, para. 1). A perfect display of these skills occurred when an individual came to a nurse-managed clinic after her back pain was unrelieved by medications prescribed by her physician. After performing a thorough physical assessment, the nurse listened as the client told of financial stress and sleeping in her bathtub to ensure all other family members had a bed. The nurse helped the individual find larger, affordable housing and a suitable place to sleep. Subsequently, the back pain was alleviated.

What a great example of delivery of care fully in the scope of nursing practice that does not fragment physical, mental, social, and spiritual health.

Addressing the needs of the whole person can happen anywhere. Unfortunately, current healthcare systems focus more on acute needs within acute care settings and leave little time for evaluating the person's lived experience. This whole-person care delivery happens when healthcare teams encounter the homes, schools, churches, workplaces, and gathering places of a community and see their influence on community members' health and health-related choices. We need to bring healthcare to where people are, rather than expecting those with limited time, money, transportation, perception of health needs, or knowledge of healthcare resources to actively seek healthcare.

Nurses, be ready for a healthcare revolution that focuses as much on nurse care integrators prescribing food, exercise, sleep, and basic necessities of life as on healthcare providers prescribing medications and medical tests. It is time to develop nurses as leaders in delivering care where people are, advancing a Culture of Health rather than a culture of healthcare.

"Wherever they practice, it is nurses who will determine if those in their charge will be changed positively or negatively by the experience. In hospitals, nurses are the ever-present sentinels, the action heroes who leap to intervene when problems occur. Such vigilance requires that nurses be present in adequate numbers. We now have sufficient data to show that their absence results in poor outcomes. Administrators and hospital boards that refuse to invest in an adequate and knowledgeable nursing staff are cheating those they purport to serve and merely providing lip service to the idea of quality care."

–*Maureen Shawn Kennedy,*
MA, RN, FAAN
Editor in Chief
American Journal of Nursing

References

American Nurses Association. (2010). New care delivery models in health system reform: Opportunities for nurses & their patients. ANA Issue Brief. Retrieved from http://nursingworld.org/MainMenuCategories/Policy-Advocacy/Positions-and-Resolutions/Issue-Briefs/Care-Delivery-Models.pdf

American Nurses Association. (2016). What is nursing? Retrieved from http://www.nursingworld.org/EspeciallyForYou/What-is-Nursing

Brooks, M. (2014, October). Nurse-led initiative improves VA psychiatric care. Poster session presented at the 28th annual conference of the American Psychiatric Nurses Association, Indianapolis, IN.

Joynt, J., & Kimball, B. (2008, January). Innovative care delivery models: Identifying new models that effectively leverage nurses. Retrieved from http://gsh-education.wiki.usfca.edu/file/view/HWS-RWJF-CDM-White-Paper.pdf

Lee, S., Lee, A., Lim, S., Koh, M., Tan, B., Phan, P., ... Fisher, D. (2014). A pilot study on nurse-led rounds: Preliminary data on patient contact time. *Internal Journal of Technical Research and Applications, 2*(Special Issue 5), 68–71. e-ISSN: 2320–8163

Nolte, E., & McKee, M. (2011). Variations in amenable mortality—Trends in 16 high-income nations. *Health Policy, 103*(1), 47–52. doi:10.1016/j.healthpol.2011.08.002

World Health Organization. (2013). Global health expenditure database. Retrieved from http://apps.who.int/nha/database/ViewData/Indicators/en

"It is truly a unique time to be a nurse. Healthcare reform literally begs for nurses to work to the 'top of their license'—whether a registered nurse or advanced practice nurse. It is so critical to deliver comprehensive, compassionate, and coordinated care for our patients and their families. Consumers depend upon our largest and most trusted healthcare workforce members—registered nurses. Delivering the very best care possible, and supporting that care delivery everywhere, is the challenge posed by improved access, increased quality, and reduced cost. Nurses can, do, and will meet these challenges head-on!"

–Ann Scott Blouin, RN, PhD, FACHE
Executive Vice President, Customer Relations
Certified Green Belt
The Joint Commission

Priority #10: Professional Handoff

In this section:

- The Dance of Mentorship
- Nurse Esteem

Mentoring and professional handoff have never been more important than right now. With baby boomers retiring, the nursing profession will feel a deep loss of wisdom and knowledge. However, with the right programs and intentions, through mentoring and strategic handoffs, the profession can weather this wisdom drain unscathed. This calls for each nurse, regardless of years of experience, novice or expert, to seek to be mentored and to be a mentee. Mentoring for a professional handoff does not mean telling others what to do and how to do it. This is about sharing insights and wisdom gained on a personal journey that might be helpful to others on their own professional journey.

How are you positively contributing to the handoff of our profession to the future? As you read the essays about professional handoff, reflect on the following questions and issues:

1. How do we enable senior nurses to move into more supportive roles—helping to create opportunity and lift those coming up?

2. How do we assist those nearing retirement who don't see the next step and are clinging to the last—can we learn from other disciplines?

3. Can we create wisdom circles? How can we engage senior members of the profession in mentoring newer members and in contributing to broad solutions in health?

"In order to meet the needs of our organization's growing nurse population, we launched a mentoring program called iNspire (Inspiring Nurse Success and Partnership in Reaching Excellence). The annual cohort-based program goals are to improve nurse retention; engagement; business acumen; cross-segment networking; and nurse personal, professional, and leadership development. A critical factor in the program is the match of the mentee with the mentor, as the relationship of sharing sage advice with the mentee allows for future generations to learn from their mentors. We have found the mentee promotion rate is 26% higher than our overall nurse population. Mentoring in nursing leads to many rewards for the mentee, mentor, and organization."

–Mary Jo Jerde, MBA, BSN, NEA-BC, RN-BC
Senior Vice President, Center for Clinician Advancement
UnitedHealth Group

4. How do we encourage all nurses to mentor and help each other with the understanding that this will benefit individuals they care for?

5. How can we ensure the "new generation" of nurses is prepared to fill roles as baby boomers retire? Hospitals aren't investing in new graduates. How can we solve this problem?

6. How do we transfer knowledge and wisdom among generations of nurses, allowing the experienced to share their wisdom and insight, while allowing the upcoming generations to forge their own paths?

The Dance of Mentorship

–Diana Ruiz, DNP, RN, APHN-BC, CWOCN, NE-BC, CHW

Diana Ruiz
*Director of Community Health
Medical Center Health System
(overseeing two of the system's
Texas Medicaid 1115
Waiver projects, the Care Transition
Program, and the Faith & Health
Network)*

As I reflect on the beginning of my nursing education, I vividly recall wanting to enter healthcare to help others and to advance my own knowledge. I don't think I realized the amazing journey I was embarking on. I never imagined that I would enter such a renowned and respected profession.

While my initial education was great and laid the foundation on which to build, my true passion in nursing leadership was ignited while pursuing a graduate degree. At that point, I first encountered mentors—nurse leaders with a phenomenal amount of education, experience, and wisdom who were actually willing to invest in me. Throughout my nearly 13 years as a nurse, I have been supported, challenged, and empowered by some of the most amazing nurse leaders in this country. The key similarity in each of these mentors was their selfless willingness to contribute to the next generation of nurses.

While they were focused on me and my growth, I began to shift my focus to others. I felt the need to pay it forward, even though I had by no means arrived in my career. I have worked at an amazing healthcare system for my entire career and have always been surrounded by great nurses. Yet I was driven to help challenge and inspire them in the same ways that others had done for me. Together we have grown, advanced our education, challenged the status quo, and led system-wide initiatives that will impact patient care for years to come.

What must our current profession do to advance health and make an impact in generations to come? The answers are quite simple. First, invest in others; the dividend will be tremendous. Be the spark that ignites others to be more, do more, and serve more. Make a concerted effort to mentor those who are starving for guidance from the wisdom circle of nurses before them. Second, make a commitment to find a mentor. Finding a mentor is best accomplished through engagement in professional networks and initiatives such as the Future of Nursing: Campaign for Action and state-based and specialty organizations. Diversity may best be found beyond your immediate workplace, in some cases to enhance the mentorship experience. The art of mentoring has long been supported in many fields, and in a profession with such a societal influence as nursing, we must be purposeful about our role in promoting a Culture of Health.

Mentoring is a beautiful dance in which sometimes you lead and sometimes you follow. A successful mentor/mentee relationship involves time commitment, a pact to challenge and encourage one another, and mutually beneficial goals for all. Ideally, the relationship continues to strengthen over time and evolves into a professional partnership. Newer generations of nurses deserve to be nurtured and given time to forge their own paths and create their own professional vision. They need to feel independent as worthy contributors to the profession and not live directly under the proverbial shadow of great leaders. Rather, experienced nurse leaders can best mentor others by inspiring and challenging them to let go of the past and move forward with a greater, system-wide vision. Best mentors are those with grace, sage advice, and willingness to allow newer nurses to learn by experience, mistakes, and personal reflection. Successful mentorships in nursing will ultimately advance our profession, the way in which we deliver care, and the way in which we lead in academics, practice, and leadership arenas.

While I have chosen mentors in my career, I have also been incredibly fortunate that many have chosen me. They have opened doors and opportunities for me that I never thought possible. Unknowingly, just by their trust, they have ignited my passion and propelled me into a new level of nursing. I can only aspire to make the same impact on future generations of nurse leaders. My best contribution to our profession will be in leading and following in the mentoring dance with students, nurses, colleagues, and other healthcare providers.

"The concept of mentoring is overused. Coaching or encouragement from a respected peer is not mentoring. A true mentor invests holistically for an expanded time frame, offering feedback that shapes a mentee's future. A mentor molds, probes, models for, and questions until the mentee discovers and acts on new insights."

–*Michael R. Bleich, PhD, RN, FAAN*
President and CEO
NursDynamics, LLC

" Nursing, like other professions, spends way too much time talking about the process of mentoring rather than actually making a difference. In fact, we could be holding the profession back by recommending outdated strategies and advice that don't work in the world of today or tomorrow. Mentoring must be a highly active, focused, intentional, episodic activity with a clearly defined purpose and goal: Improve healthcare for every person and change the world! "

–Darlene J. Curley, MS, RN
Chief Executive Officer, Jonas Family Fund
Executive Director, Jonas Center

Nurse Esteem

–Terrie P. Sterling, MSN, MBA, RN

Terrie Sterling
Chief Operating Officer
Our Lady of the Lake
Regional Medical Center
Baton Rouge, Louisiana

In 1984, Patricia Benner warned of the risk of losing the best and brightest who once considered nursing to alternative career choices. However, with the exception of 2001, in the aftermath of the 9/11 attack when firefighters topped the list, nursing has ranked first in the Gallup poll of America's professions for honesty and ethical standards since being included in the survey in 1999 (Riffkin, 2014). In our fast-paced, technically advanced environment, the work of caring for the human condition continues to have value. As nurses, we are invited into the most private moments of the lives of patients and families. As trusted partners in the healthcare delivery system, nurses often serve as navigators supporting critical decision making. In Nightingale's *Notes on Nursing* (1969), the foundation for nursing as a scientific profession was established, formalizing nursing practice and moving nursing away from the role of domestic caretaker to the prestigious profession it is today.

As nurses, we must place value on what we do from the bedside to the boardroom. Nurses are the keeper of the keys related to the public perception of this sacred profession, and we must challenge ourselves to share what is going well in our profession.

When I reflect on my nursing career, possessing a positive intrinsic value of nursing made a vast difference as a student nurse, a nurse manager, and now as a nurse executive. During my first clinical rotation in nursing school, I had a young instructor who made learning simple tasks important. As a student in a long-term care setting, learning basic activities of daily living, I still remember my instructor pulling me aside and explaining why giving a bed bath was important to an incapacitated elderly gentleman. She spoke of the patient with great dignity and respect and made me feel equally valued to have the privilege to render his care.

Later in my career, a director of nursing taught me the essence of leadership and why leading others—though challenging—was special. Through her leadership, I was volunteered for hospital committees and expected to be involved in both internal and external activities that benefited nursing, the organization, and my professional development. She spent time coaching young nurse leaders like me on the importance of nurses having a voice—not only to shape our healthcare organization but also to serve as positive catalysts in the community. We were so proud when the chief nursing officer of our organization became a member of the Rotary Club more than 20 years ago. When I attend meetings at that same Rotary Club and I'm recognized as both a nurse and member of the business community, I am reminded that so many nurses have paved the way for us.

Today, I believe we continue to underestimate the significance of being part of the global dialogue about nursing, healthcare, and the needs of our community.

Healthcare leaders grappling with cost management are piloting models of innovation and accountable care in delivery systems. Leaders are making decisions that will impact the environment in which we and future nurses practice.

As nurses, are we prepared academically, emotionally, and socially to influence healthcare at the bedside and beyond? Every nurse can and should contribute to maintaining the current esteem that exists for nursing, while elevating nursing professional practice to new heights. As a member of the most trusted profession in America, each of us is responsible for the perception we leave behind. How will talented young people learn about the multitude of opportunities in nursing? Whether in a clinical setting, classroom, or boardroom, the future of nursing rests with us. It is incumbent upon us to answer the call to serve as a catalyst for a positive nursing future that ensures the current level of respect and admiration. That challenge begins with every nurse radiating a positive self-image of nursing and the willingness to proudly tell the world, "I am a nurse!"

References

Benner, P. (1984). *From novice to expert: Excellence and power in clinical nursing practice*. Upper Saddle River, NJ: Prentice Hall Health.

Nightingale, F. (1969). *Notes on nursing: What it is and what it is not*. New York, NY: Dover Publications Inc.

Riffkin, R. (2014, December 18). Americans rate nurses highest on honesty, ethical standards. Retrieved from http://www.gallup.com/poll/180260/americans-rate-nurses-highest-honely-ethical-standards.aspx

"The 21st century requires flexibility and adaptability to keep pace with the ever-changing landscape of education and healthcare reform. Merging experience and innovation, nurse leaders intentionally share their wisdom and insights as mentors to bright, young school nurses. Leaders of today, and in our case school nurses, are accountable for building the bridge for the leaders of tomorrow so that all children can have better learning through better health."

–*Donna Mazyck, MS, RN, NCSN, CAE*
Executive Director
National Association of School Nurses

"I believe ownership of one's personal and professional goals to be a key ingredient to one's professional success and fulfillment. 'Ownership' of one's professional development and career planning, however, are not accomplished in a solitary fashion. You can, and should, solicit input from a wide variety of individuals. That's where mentorship comes into play. Mentoring relationships come in many different forms: formal to informal, young to old, short-term to long-term. As one wise mentor of mine mentioned, "A mentor does not need to look like you," personally or professionally. What really matters is that each participant is committed to the relationship: to sharing, to learning, to growing. I believe the officer who desires mentorship has a responsibility to seek out a mentor. In selecting a mentor, I recommend one who has achieved success and whose personal and professional knowledge, skills, and abilities you admire. I also believe that senior officers and more "seasoned" professional staff have a responsibility to prepare those who follow in their footsteps and to give generously of their time in mentoring others."

–Rebecca J. McCormick-Boyle
Nurse Corps, United States Navy

Afterword

Julie Fairman
*Nightingale Professor of Nursing
Chair, Department of Biobehavioral
Health Sciences
Director Emerita, Barbara Bates
Center for the Study of the History
of Nursing*

As a historian, I find writing an afterword to be the ultimate honor and challenge. Historians examine change over time and then help explain that change in terms of present understanding and future thinking. After reading the essays in this volume, one gets a sense of déjà vu: We have been here before. As my mentor Joan Lynaugh would say to me, "Everything has a past." None of the issues we face as a profession today is new, but the issues are presented here in a very different context that focuses on patient care rather than professional interest. Each author has used the context of the present and also indirectly embedded the past as a way to examine his or her area of expertise. It is in this vein that I will take this opportunity to look forward but also to see the historical nature of our ideas, as well as the opportunities and challenges we face as nurses working to improve the health of the nation.

At least two themes are threaded throughout this collection of essays: the concept of voice and the importance of a Culture of Health. Both are intertwined and infused with historical significance and future possibilities. Everyone has "voice"—the public, providers, policymakers, insurers, and many others—but there are many factors that influence how, when, and if their voice is heard or if dominant powers listen. The public has voice, and we hear it in voting trends and through protests as well as during debates about how much healthcare costs and how it should be provided. The public supports nurse practitioners; public voice helped make nurse practitioners respected providers. Public voice is not homogenous—sometimes public voice is for the greater good, and sometimes it is protective toward particular groups. Voice can be exclusive or inclusive. Sometimes voice is muted, depending on socioeconomic status, geography, gender, race/ethnicity, or religion. The characteristics and values of those in power many times determine who is listened to and when.

Public polls situate nurses as the most trusted health professionals. This is indeed a powerful voice from the perspective of both the public and nurses, but it does come with great responsibility. The public sees nurses as expert caregivers, as advocates, and as true normative providers in roles traditionally owned by physicians. As the essays point out, nurses provide care across the continuum, from health promotion and disease prevention to hospice care for the dying. Nurses must in turn see the public—individual patients, families, and communities—as partners in developing better models and systems of care that are responsive to public needs. Nurses' leadership is greatly needed to work with the public, be it on the board of a hospital or community center, and to lead these changes. All of the emerging leaders in these essays also speak to mentors who helped them grow to gain their own voice as well as more clearly hear the voice of the public.

The relationship between nurses and the public is historically continuous but also contextual. It is shaped by time and place. Nurses have participated in questionable, and sometimes harmful, research studies; supported segregation; and excluded those who were not white, middle-class women from becoming nurses. This is our history, and it is important to understand and to know it. On the other hand, nurses are indispensable during disasters or epidemics and have a tradition of going to places that physicians or other providers will not go or have little interest. In Flint, Michigan, a public health nurse helped to sound the alarm on lead exposure in the community. During flu epidemics, nurses provided the only therapy that kept patients safe and comfortable. Lillian Wald, along with Mary Brewster, established the Henry Street Settlement House in New York City in 1893. In her earlier practice, Wald saw the oppressive circumstances of poor immigrants on the lower east side of Manhattan and began the Nurses' Settlement to bring together and address the needs of this community for better housing, education, jobs, and health education and promotion. In an interesting example of helping people transition across systems, Settlement nurses also followed patients across institutions, homes, and schools to make sure the right instructions were transmitted and understood after a physician visit or after hospitalization. There are many examples of nurses helping communities to obtain health services as well as to address issues such as poverty, safety, housing, and good nutrition.

We sometimes must carefully ensure that public voice is prioritized over the voices of the professions. We do know that nurses' efforts to provide care to the public are sometimes paternalistic and more a reflection of professional prerogative than community preference or need. Sometimes we fail to engage the community in our plans but infuse our message with the politics of nation-building or the gospel of science. This is another historic continuity. For example, nursing historian Patricia D'Antonio writes about the political battles between nurses and city organizations that defeated the Harlem Demonstration Project, a public health initiative, in the early 1920s. In the global context, nurses' efforts to "civilize" and bring the gospel of science to colonized populations at times disrespected local customs and beliefs, or their efforts were structured to gain public loyalty during times of insurgencies or uprisings against colonial rule. But we also see the beauty in community engagement to address social determinants to build a Culture of Health. Nurse-managed health centers like the Stephen and Sandra Sheller 11th Street Family Health Services of Drexel University and Ruth Lubic's Developing Families Center, which engaged the community from the development phase, are able to maximize their impact. But these centers, both located in areas of high levels of poverty, crime, and infant and maternal mortality, cannot thrive until they have a dedicated funding source and the political environment is conducive to support these models.

Part of the struggle for the nursing profession is to understand how to help amplify the voice of those who are most affected by social determinants and to respond in a way that respects their voice—to create a Culture of Health. As some of the essays in this volume point out, education and expert practice are critical to ensuring public trust and listening to public voice. The Institute of Medicine's seminal report on *The Future of Nursing: Leading Change, Transforming Health* explicitly laid out the need for nurses to have a broad understanding of health and to see the connections among health, income, race, gender, and other social determinants. The report recommended that nurses pursue higher education, not for parochial professional advancement but to gain the skills to integrate this broader vision into their practice in a reformed health system to better serve the public. The report also emphasized the need to diversify the nursing workforce, to offer opportunities for voice that entry into the nursing profession brings to many different groups of people. Diversity by race/ethnicity, gender, and other categories also brings voice to patients as the nursing workforce gains a greater capacity to understand the needs of our citizens when they are most vulnerable and sick.

Nurses should be and are at the forefront during this period of incredible innovation and reform. This is truly nursing's time to respond to and keep the public's trust and to move forward an agenda of reform and public engagement. The profession's historic paradigm of caregiving across time and place provides legitimacy for its positionality. But, as Martin Luther King Jr. noted, "True compassion is more than flinging a coin to a beggar; it is not haphazard and superficial. It comes to see that an edifice that produces beggars needs restructuring." Nurses do need the skills and knowledge they gain from higher education to take on leadership roles; to make the clinical connections between, for example, someone's home environment and his or her mental health; to create the models of care that directly engage the public in a Culture of Health and provide the space for the public's voice to be heard. And, we need to partner and show others why it is imperative for them to partner with us and the public to improve health.

This is nursing's historic challenge and opportunity. The health of our most vulnerable citizens determines our nation's and our world's health. Access to quality healthcare has become more than a luxury—it is a civil right. Again, to quote Dr. King, "Of all the forms of inequality, injustice in healthcare is the most shocking and inhumane." Together with citizen partners, physicians, educators, philanthropic foundations, insurers and many other stakeholders, nursing is well-situated to lead change and support a Culture of Health. Nurses need to have the skills to hear, to listen, to lead, and to act to ensure that all citizens are heard and have access to high quality healthcare.

–Julie A. Fairman, PhD, RN, FAAN

A Call to Action

As our profession grows in numbers, our perspectives broaden with our diversity of experiences and thought. Bringing the profession together around ten powerful issues has the opportunity to build bridges among ourselves, and start meaning conversations, whether we practice nursing in the United States, or around the world.

Do not simply consider this a book of perspectives. Consider this a call to action. A call that stimulated your own thoughts, ideas, and resolve to strengthen the profession. How will you embrace the Culture of Health? How do you see the Culture of Health and each of these ten issues coming together? What do you see as the answers to these ten issues? What wisdom and insight will you leave for the following generations on these issues? Who will you mentor and who will you ask to be a mentor to you?

We hope that you have enjoyed reading the essays from some of the many great sages and young leaders in nursing. As this was an update to the original book published five years ago, we felt it was important to continue to drive the idea of ten. Ten power issues in nursing that have the power to change the world. Florence Nightingale changed the world over 130 years ago, yet she was just *one nurse*. We are all just *one nurse* as well, one that can change tomorrow, and what our future generations will know 130 years from now, just like Florence did.

—Sue & Jennifer

Acknowledgments

In order to create a book like this, we knew we needed to get as much input from as diverse of a group of nursing leaders as we could, and our search took us not only across the country, but globally. This book was truly co-created, with the knowledge, expertise, wisdom, and guidance of many. Some individuals contributed in essays and quotes, others helped during the brainstorming phase. This brainstorming allowed us to determine the top themes that you will read about throughout this book. We want to acknowledge their insight and wisdom, which has paved the way for our profession for decades. And for their insight and wisdom, which will continue to guide generations of nurses to come.

Thank you for contributing your wisdom.

Susan Hassmiller

About the Author

Susan B. Hassmiller, PhD, RN, FAAN, joined the Robert Wood Johnson Foundation (RWJF) in 1997 and is presently the Robert Wood Johnson Foundation Senior Adviser for Nursing. In this role, she shapes and leads the Foundation's nursing strategies in an effort to create a higher quality of care in the United States for people, families, and communities. Drawn to the Foundation's "organizational advocacy for the less fortunate and underserved," Hassmiller is helping to assure that RWJF's commitments in nursing have a broad and lasting national impact. In partnership with AARP, Hassmiller directs the Foundation's Future of Nursing: Campaign for Action, which seeks to ensure that everyone in America can live a healthier life, supported by a system in which nurses are essential partners in providing care and promoting health. This 50-state and District of Columbia effort strives to implement the recommendations of the Institute of Medicine's report on the *Future of Nursing: Leading Change, Advancing Health.* Hassmiller served as the report's study director. She is also serving as Co-Director of the Future of Nursing Scholars program, an initiative that provides scholarships, mentoring and leadership development activities and postdoctoral research funding to build the leadership capacity of nurse educators and researchers.

Previously, Hassmiller served with the Health Resources and Services Administration, where she was the Executive Director of the U.S. Public Health Service Primary Care Policy Fellowship and worked on other national and international primary care initiatives. She also has worked in public health settings at the local and state level and taught public health nursing at the University of Nebraska and George Mason University in Virginia.

Hassmiller, who has been very involved with the Red Cross in many capacities, was a member of the National Board of Governors for the American Red Cross, serving as chair of the Disaster and Chapter Services Committee and National Chair of the 9/11 Recovery Program. She is currently a member of the National Nursing Committee, and is serving as Immediate Past Board Chair for the Central New Jersey Red Cross. She has been involved in Red Cross disaster relief efforts in the United States and abroad, including tornadoes in the Midwest, Hurricane Andrew, September 11th, the 2004 Florida hurricanes and Katrina, and the tsunami in Indonesia. Hassmiller is a member of the Institute of Medicine, a fellow in the American Academy of Nursing, a member of the Joint Commission's National Nurse Advisory Council, Meridian Health System Board of Directors, the Health Resources and Services Administration National Advisory Committee for Nurse Education and Practice, and the CMS National Nurse Steering Committee.

Hassmiller received a PhD in nursing administration and health policy from George Mason University in Fairfax, Virginia, master's degrees in health education from Florida State University and community health nursing from the University of Nebraska Medical Center, and a bachelor's degree in nursing from

Florida State University. She is the recipient of numerous national awards in addition to receiving the distinguished alumna award for all the schools of nursing from which she graduated and two honorary doctoral degrees. Most notably, Hassmiller is the 2009 recipient of the Florence Nightingale Medal, the highest international honor given to a nurse by the International Committee of the Red Cross.

About the Author

Jennifer Mensik

Jennifer S. Mensik, PhD, RN, NEA-BC, FAAN, is Executive Director of Nursing, Medicine, and Pharmacy Programs for OnCourse Learning and faculty for Arizona State University College of Nursing and Health Innovation DNP and undergraduate programs. She earned a PhD in nursing from the University of Arizona College of Nursing with a major focus in health systems and a minor in public administration from the Eller College of Management. She has extensive leadership experience, including employment as Administrator for Nursing and Patient Care at a Magnet-designated health system, Executive Director of Quality and Patient Safety, and System Director of Clinical Practice and Research. Mensik has authored numerous publications, including the books *Lead, Drive, and Thrive in the System* and *The Nurse Manager's Guide to Innovative Staffing*. She is a co-author of *A Nurse's Step-By-Step Guide to Transitioning to the Professional Nurse Role* and a chapter author for *The Career Handoff: A Healthcare Leader's Guide to Knowledge & Wisdom Transfer Across Generations*.

She has served as President of the Arizona Nurses Association and has also served nationally for the American Nurses Association as Second Vice President and Director at Large on the board of directors. Mensik has published and presented nationally and regionally on quality, staffing, and professional practice and is an article reviewer for *Nursing Outlook*, *Worldviews on Evidence-Based Nursing*, and *Nursing Economic$*.

Lucia Alfano p. 26

Linda Burnes Bolton
p. 94

About the Contributing Authors

Lucia J. Alfano, MA, RN, is an expert public health nurse and nurse educator with more than 14 years of experience in community leadership. She currently serves as nursing faculty at Concordia College in New York and as a public health nurse at Sterling Home Care in Connecticut. She is a well-known change agent and founder of programs and services to help advance health and support healthcare systems. She has primarily focused on mentorship, diversity, and advocacy. Alfano volunteers her time as co-chair for tactical support and operations for the Future of Nursing: NYS Action Coalition, an Action Coalition that is part of the national Future of Nursing: Campaign for Action, supported by Robert Wood Johnson Foundation and AARP. She is a member of a governing board for a large community health organization in New York City. A longtime member of the National Association of Hispanic Nurses, she is the founding President of NAHN Westchester.

Linda Burnes Bolton, DrPH, RN, FAAN, is System Chief Nurse Executive, Vice President of Nursing, Chief Nursing Officer, and Director of Nursing Research at Cedars-Sinai Medical Center in Los Angeles, California. She is a principal investigator at the Cedars-Sinai Burns & Allen Research Institute. She holds board appointments with the Robert Wood Johnson Foundation and HealthImpact of California and is a trustee of Case Western Reserve University. She earned her undergraduate degree from Arizona State University School of Nursing in 1970. She holds a master's in nursing, a master's in public health, and a doctorate in public health from University of California Los Angeles. She was awarded an honorary doctor of science degree from the State University of New York in 2015. Burnes Bolton is a Past President of the American Academy of Nursing, National Black Nurses Association, and the American Organization of Nurse Executives. She was appointed to the National Academy of Medicine in 2015.

Garrett K. Chan, PhD, APRN, FAEN, FPCN, FNAP, FAAN, is Director of Advanced Practice at Stanford Health Care and Clinical Associate Professor in the Division of General Medical Disciplines and the Department of Emergency Medicine at Stanford University School of Medicine. He is responsible for the professional practice of advanced practice providers (APPs), which include nurse practitioners, physician assistants, clinical nurse specialists, and certified registered nurse anesthetists. His research and clinical practice focus on palliative care in emergency care as well as the impact of advanced practice providers on health outcomes and policy. Chan received his BSN from San José State University and his master's and PhD from the University of California, San Francisco. He is an elected fellow of the Academy of Emergency Nursing, Hospice and Palliative Nurses Association, National Academies of Practice, and American Academy of Nursing.

Garrett Chan p. 128

Marilyn P. Chow, PhD, RN, FAAN, is Vice President of National Patient Care Services and Innovation at Kaiser Permanente, where she works to enable the delivery of the highest quality and most safe patient-centered care. She has made significant contributions to nursing through her scholarship, leadership, and civic involvement. She is recognized for her expertise in innovation, regulation of nursing practice, and workforce policy. Chow is committed to incorporating innovation and technology to reduce waste and improve workflows within the healthcare industry. She was the driving force in conceptualizing and creating the Sidney R. Garfield Health Care Innovation Center, Kaiser Permanente's living laboratory, where ideas are tested and solutions are developed in a hands-on, simulated clinical environment. She was the inaugural Program Director for the RWJF Executive Nurse Fellows Program and is currently chair of the Institute of Medicine's Standing Committee on Credentialing Research in Nursing. In 2003, Chow participated on the IOM Committee that produced the report *Keeping Patients Safe: Transforming the Work Environment of Nurses*. She is a current board member of the California Institute for Nursing and Health Care (CINHC), the Innovation Learning Network, and the Kaiser Permanente Sidney R. Garfield Health Care Innovation Center. She is the recipient of numer-

Marilyn Chow pp. 4, 19

Margaret Flinter
p. 133

Elizabeth Holguin
p. 114

ous awards, including the American Organization of Nurse Executives (AONE) 2013 Lifetime Achievement Award; the 2013 HIT Men and Women Award, presented by Healthcare IT News; and the national Nurse.com 2011 Nursing Excellence, National Nurse of the Year. She also was selected as one of the distinguished 100 graduates and faculty of the UCSF School of Nursing for the Centennial Wall of Fame.

Margaret Flinter, APRN, PhD, C-FNP, FAAN, FAANP, is Senior Vice President and Clinical Director of the Community Health Center Inc. and is board certified as a family nurse practitioner. She earned her bachelor's degree in nursing from the University of Connecticut, her master's degree from Yale University, and her PhD from the University of Connecticut. She was the recipient of a Robert Wood Johnson Executive Nurse Fellowship from 2002-05. Following her graduate training at Yale University, Flinter joined the Community Health Center in 1980 as a National Health Service Corps Scholar and CHC's first nurse practitioner. Since 1987 she has held both clinical and executive leadership positions in the organization. She established the Weitzman Center, now known as the Weitzman Institute, in 2015 and established the United State's first postgraduate NP residency program for primary care NPs in 2007. Flinter also serves as national Co-Director of the LEAP (Learning from Effective Ambulatory Practices) project and is co-principal investigator of the HRSA National Cooperative Agreement on Clinical Workforce Development.

Elizabeth Holguin, MPH, MSN, FNP-BC, is a doctoral student at the University of New Mexico in nursing and health policy. She is a Robert Wood Johnson Foundation Nursing and Health Policy Collaborative Fellow and a Jonas Nurse Leader Scholar. She received her master's of public health from Tulane University as a master's international student and served in the Peace Corps in Ethiopia. During her graduate studies, she also implemented an infection control program in a government hospital in Kenema, Sierra Leone, West Africa. She then received a master's of science in nursing degree from Duke University and became certified as a family nurse practitioner. She combined her passion for neurosurgery and public health by managing a research program dedicated to reducing transport to a level one trauma center and increasing access to specialty care with telemedicine with a focus on mild traumatic brain injuries for Indian Health Service hospitals. Current research interests include increasing access to care and resource sustainability through policy implementation at the national and global level and feasibility and cost-effectiveness of healthcare coverage for undocumented immigrants.

Frances Hughes, DNurs, RN, Col (ret), JP, ONZM, was appointed Chief Executive Officer of the International Council of Nurses in February 2016. Immediately prior to this, she was Chief Nursing and Midwifery Officer, Queensland, Australia, and also served as Chief Nurse for New Zealand. From 2005-11, Hughes worked for the World Health Organization with 16 countries in the Pacific region, supporting them to develop policy and plans to improve mental health for consumers in the Pacific. Qualified as a general and psychiatric health nurse, Hughes has a doctor of nursing degree from the University of Technology, Sydney. She has held senior roles for many years across a range of organizations and served as Commandant Colonel for the Royal New Zealand Nursing Corps. Hughes has an extensive publication record and has received several awards for her work.

Frances Hughes
p. 100

Jesse M. L. Kennedy, BSN, RN, is a staff nurse in the intensive care unit at PeaceHealth Sacred Heart Medical Center at RiverBend in Oregon. He is serving in his second term as Director at Large, Recent Graduate on the American Nurses Association board of directors. He is also a staff nurse in the intensive care unit at PeaceHealth Sacred Heart Medical Center at RiverBend in Oregon. He previously served as President of the National Student Nurses' Association and Vice President of the Oregon Student Nurses' Association. Kennedy graduated with his ADN from Lane Community College and his BSN from Oregon Health and Sciences University. He has been a vocal advocate for nursing leadership and served on numerous task forces and councils at the national, state, and local level focused on leadership development, recent graduate development, scope of practice, and legislation/policy development. Kennedy also has practiced leadership development directly by organizing vaccination clinics and two nursing

Jesse Kennedy
p. 104

Beverly Malone p. 46

Suzanne Miyamoto
p. 79

brigade volunteer missions to Thailand, by developing a nurse residency program at his facility, and through direct mentoring. He is also the founder of Nurse Connect, a group aimed at building camaraderie among nurses and facilitating mentorship opportunities.

Beverly Malone, PhD, RN, FAAN, is Chief Executive Officer of the National League for Nursing (NLN). Her tenure at NLN has been marked by a retooling of the league's mission to reflect the core values of caring, diversity, integrity, and excellence and an ongoing focus on advancing the health of the nation and the global community. She was ranked among the 100 Most Powerful People in Healthcare by *Modern Healthcare* magazine in 2010 and 2015. Within the last several years, Malone was elected to the Institute of Medicine and tapped to join the board of the Kaiser Family Foundation. She served on the Institute of Medicine's Forum on the Future of Nursing Education, contributing to the IOM's groundbreaking report *The Future of Nursing: Leading Change, Advancing Health*, and on the Advisory Committee on Minority Health, a federal panel established to advise the U.S. Secretary of Health and Human Services. Her distinguished career has mixed policy, education, administration, and clinical practice. Malone has worked as a surgical staff nurse, clinical nurse specialist, Director of Nursing, and Assistant Administrator of Nursing. During the 1980s, she was Dean of the School of Nursing at North Carolina Agricultural and Technical State University. In 1996, she was elected to two terms as President of the American Nurses Association (ANA), representing 180,000 nurses in the USA. In 2000, she became Deputy Assistant Secretary for Health within the U.S. Department of Health and Human Services. Just prior to joining the NLN, Malone was General Secretary of the Royal College of Nursing (RCN), the United Kingdom's largest professional union of nurses, from June 2001 to January 2007.

Suzanne Miyamoto, PhD, RN, FAAN, is Senior Director of Government Affairs and Health Policy at the American Association of Colleges of Nursing (AACN). With over a decade of policy experience, Miyamoto leads the association's policy and advocacy work focused on advancing nursing education, research, and practice to promote a cost-effective, high quality healthcare system. She is the Convener for the Nursing Community, a coalition of 62 national nursing organizations that collaborate on a wide spectrum of health policy issues. Miyamoto is a 2014 Robert Wood Johnson Foundation Executive Nurse Fellow and Adjunct Assistant Professor at Georgetown University School of Nursing and Health Studies. Previously, she held policy positions at the state and federal level with the National Institutes of Health and the State Commission on Patient Safety for the Michigan Health and Safety Coalition. Miyamoto received her degrees from the University of Michigan, Ann Arbor, School of Nursing.

Mary D. Naylor, PhD, RN, FAAN, is the Marian S. Ware Professor in Gerontology and Director of the NewCourtland Center for Transitions and Health at the University of Pennsylvania School of Nursing. For the past 2 decades, Naylor has led an interdisciplinary program of research designed to improve quality of care, decrease unnecessary hospitalizations, and reduce healthcare costs for vulnerable community-based elders. For 8 years, Naylor served as the National Program Director of the Robert Wood Johnson Foundation Interdisciplinary Nursing Quality Research Initiative, which was aimed at generating, disseminating. and translating research to understand how nurses contribute to quality patient care. She was elected to the National Academy of Medicine in 2005 and is a member of the Leadership Consortium on Value & Science-Driven Health Care. She co-chairs the Care Culture and Decision-making Innovation Collaborative. Naylor also is a member of the ABIM Foundation Board of Trustees, RAND Health Board of Advisors, and Agency for Healthcare Research and Quality National Advisory Council. She recently completed her term on the National Quality Forum Board of Directors. She was appointed to the Medicare Payment Advisory Commission in 2010.

Danielle Howa Pendergrass, DNP, APRN, WHNP-BC, is President of Eastern Utah Women's Health, LLC. She is a board certified women's health nurse practitioner with 12 years of clinical experience and over 19 years of nursing experience. In 2013, she earned her DNP from the University of Utah. She owns and operates Eastern Utah Women's Health in rural Price, Utah. Pendergrass is one of 20 nurses named as a Breakthrough Leader in Nursing by

Mary Naylor p. 83

Danielle Howa
Pendergrass p. 15

Adriana Perez p. 52

Stephen Perez p. 63

the Future of Nursing: Campaign for Action, a joint initiative of AARP and the Robert Wood Johnson Foundation. She was featured in AARP, is the recipient of two state leadership awards, and was recently honored with the Nurse Practitioner in Women's Health Inspirations award. She serves as the Utah State Representative for the American Association of Nurse Practitioners. Pendergrass plans to continue her work with the RWJF, AARP, AANP, and the Utah Action Coalition for Health to build a Culture of Health in her community and throughout the nation.

G. Adriana Perez, PhD, ANP-BC, FAAN, is an Assistant Professor at the University of Pennsylvania School of Nursing and serves as consultant for the Diversity Steering Committee at the Center to Champion Nursing in America. Her innovative contributions to cardiovascular health promotion among older Latinas, in partnership with nonprofits and community leaders, includes development and testing of a wellness motivation intervention for physical activity funded by the John A. Hartford Foundation National Hartford Centers of Gerontological Nursing Excellence through a pre- and post-doctoral fellowship; NIH/NINR through an Individual Nursing Research Service Award; National Coalition of Ethnic Minority Nurses; and St. Luke's Health Initiative. She was competitively selected as Health and Aging Policy Fellow and the Centers for Disease Control & Prevention Healthy Aging Program Fellow. Perez is the current principal investigator for one of 13 national grants through the Partnerships to Increase Coverage in Communities Initiative funded by the U.S. Department of Health & Human Services, Office of Minority Health.

Stephen Perez, MS, RN, ANP-BC, ACRN, is a doctoral student at the University of Pennsylvania, where he was named a Robert Wood Johnson Foundation Future of Nursing Scholar. His current research focuses on the implications of public policy on infectious diseases, particularly healthcare-associated infections. Perez has been a practicing nurse practitioner in HIV care since 2009 and served as a quality improvement consultant for the Inova Juniper Program, the largest provider of HIV services in Northern Virginia. In this role, he led the interdisciplinary quality improvement program to national recognition from the National Quality Center. He has served as the lead clinician on a national capacity-building project to train community health center providers and administrators in HIV-related clinical care and performance improvement. He maintains an active consulting practice as a clinician and performance improvement specialist. In addition to his full-time studies, he works as an Infection Preventionist and Data Analyst at the Hospital of the University of Pennsylvania

Diana Ruiz, DNP, RN, APHN-BC, CWOCN, NE-BC, CHW, is Director of Community Health at Medical Center Health System. She oversees two of the system's Texas Medicaid 1115 Waiver projects, the Care Transition Program, and the Faith & Health Network. Additionally, she leads a state-funded grant and community coalition aimed at improving overall community health and wellness. In her previous role, Ruiz served as Director of Education, helping to mentor new nurses and implementing a student-led quality improvement initiative. She also serves as contributing faculty for Grand Canyon University and the University of Texas of the Permian Basin. She is board certified as a nurse executive; advanced public health nurse; community health worker; and wound, ostomy, and continence nurse. She serves on the Odessa College Foundation Board of Directors and the ECISD School Health Advisory Council. Most recently she was honored as a 2014 Breakthrough Leader in Nursing by the Robert Wood Johnson Foundation.

Diana Ruiz p. 159

Kathleen D. Sanford, DBA, RN, FACHE, FAAN, is Senior Vice President and Chief Nursing Officer at Catholic Health Initiatives (CHI). Sanford is responsible for quality and patient safety, clinical operating improvement, leadership development, and clinical information technology at CHI. She leads evidenced-based practice initiatives and the practice of nursing across CHI's continuum. She has more than 40 years of healthcare experience as a clinician and executive. She retired from the Army as Chief Nurse of the Washington Army National Guard. She is a

Kathleen Sanford
p. 143

Judith Shamian p. 119

Terrie Sterling p. 163

past President of the American Association of Nurse Executives and a past board member of several healthcare organizations, including the American Hospital Association and Nursing Organizations Alliance. Currently Editor-In-Chief of *Nursing Administration Quarterly*, she recently co-authored *Dyad Leadership in Healthcare: When One Plus One is Greater than Two* with her dyad partner, Stephen Moore, past CHI Chief Medical Officer, as well as the management book *Leading With Love*.

Judith Shamian, PhD, RN, LLD (hon), DSci (hon), FAAN, was elected as the 27th President of the International Council of Nurses (ICN) in 2013. Shamian has over 35 years of experience in various leadership positions at local, national, and international levels. She also serves as President Emeritus, immediate past President, and CEO of a large Canadian home care organization and past President of the Canadian Nurses Association (CNA). Shamian serves on the United Nations Secretary-General's High-Level Commission on Health Employment and Economic Growth (2016), which is co-chaired by H.E. Mr. Francois Hollande, President of France, and H.E. Mr. Jacob Zuma, President of South Africa. Previously, she was a Professor of Nursing at the University of Toronto and established the Office of Nursing Policy at Health Canada. Shamian obtained her PhD from Case Western Reserve University, her master's in public health from New York University, and a baccalaureate in community nursing from Concordia University in Montreal. She is the recipient of numerous awards, including Canada's Most Powerful Women: Top 100 award; the Golden Jubilee Medal from the Governor General of Canada; and the CNA's Centennial Award. Shamian is also an international fellow with the American Academy of Nursing.

Terrie P. Sterling, MSN, MBA, RN, is Chief Operating Officer of Our Lady of the Lake Regional Medical Center in Baton Rouge, Louisiana. She is responsible for day-to-day operations at the 801-bed regional medical center, Children's Hospital, and 141-bed Heart & Vascular Institute, with a medical staff of over 1,000 members and over 6,500 employees. Sterling is a member of the Board of Directors of the Federal Reserve Bank of Atlanta's New Orleans Branch and a board member of the Capital Area American Heart Association. She is also a member of The Rotary Club of Baton Rouge. Her professional activities include membership in the Honor Society of Nursing, Sigma Theta Tau International and the American Organization of Nurse Executives. She is a fellow of the American College of Healthcare Executives. Sterling earned a BS in nursing from Northeast Louisiana University, a master's degree in nursing science from Loyola University, and an MBA from Louisiana State University.

Andrea Tanner, MSN, RN, NCSN, is a school nurse and Coordinator of Health Services at New Albany-Floyd County Schools in southern Indiana. She is a National Association of School Nurses (NASN) Epinephrine Resource School Nurse, National Certified School Nurse, and one of only 10 nationally selected 2015 Breakthrough Leaders in Nursing. Tanner received her BSN from Murray State University and MSN (school health/public health clinical nursing specialist) from the University of Missouri. She has been in school nursing for 13 years, creating a Culture of Health by connecting with students, families, and community resources; partnering with her local hospital and health department to promote physical activity and improved nutrition throughout the community; initiating programs to meet the needs of students with life-threatening allergies and drug overdose at school; providing immunization clinics in schools; and creating health education programs for students, parents, and staff. She has taught pediatric nursing and enjoys mentoring student nurses interested in community health.

Andrea Tanner
p. 189

Pamela Thompson, MS, RN, CENP, FAAN, is Chief Executive Officer of the American Organization of Nurse Executives and Senior Vice President for Nursing and Chief Nursing Officer of the American Hospital Association. She is responsible for the management and administrative leadership of AONE, as well as coordinating the AHA Workforce Initiative and addressing issues specific to strengthening the nursing workforce and redesigning patient care delivery. Before joining AONE, Thompson was Vice President of Children's Hospital, Obstetrics, Psychiatric Services, and Strategic Planning at Dartmouth-Hitchcock Medical Center in

Pamela Thompson
p. 29

Deborah Trautman
p. 36

Heather Young
pp. 9, 19

Lebanon, New Hampshire. Thompson was the recipient of the American College of Healthcare Executives 2009 Edgar C. Hayhow Award for an article she co-wrote about chief nursing officer retention and turnover. She served as chair of the National Patient Safety Foundation (NPSF) Board of Directors, was a member of the Lucien Leape Institute of NPSF, and currently serves on the NPSF Board of Advisors. Thompson was also chair of the New Hampshire Hospital Association Board of Trustees and the New Hampshire Foundation for Health Communities, as well as past President of the New Hampshire Organization of Nurse Executives. She earned her master of science degree from the University of Rochester, New York, and her bachelor of science degree from the University of Connecticut. Thompson is a fellow of the American Academy of Nursing.

Deborah E. Trautman, PhD, RN, FAAN, is President and Chief Executive Officer of the American Association of Colleges of Nursing (AACN). She joined AACN in July 2014. Prior to AACN, she served as Executive Director of the Center for Health Policy and Healthcare Transformation at Johns Hopkins Hospital. She has also served in leadership positions at the University of Pittsburgh Medical Center and the Johns Hopkins Medical Institutions. Trautman has authored publications on topics that include health policy, intimate partner violence, pain management, clinical competency, change management, cardiopulmonary bypass, and consolidation of emergency services. She is a 2007-08 Robert Wood Johnson Health Policy Fellow who worked for the Honorable Nancy Pelosi, then Speaker of the U.S. House of Representatives. Trautman received a BSN from West Virginia Wesleyan College, an MSN from the University of Pittsburgh, and a PhD in health policy from the University of Maryland, Baltimore County.

Heather M. Young, PhD, RN, FAAN, is Dignity Health Dean's Chair for Nursing Leadership; Dean and Professor, Betty Irene Moore School of Nursing; and Associate Vice Chancellor for Nursing, University of California, Davis. Young is an expert in gerontological nursing and rural healthcare. Her research and clinical interest is the promotion of healthy aging with a focus on the interface between family and formal healthcare systems. She is principal investigator of a PCORI study engaging patients and providers to improve health for individuals with diabetes and Co-Director of the UC Davis Latino Aging Research Resource Center. She was a member of the Presidential Council of Advisors on Science and Technology (PCAST) Working Group on Systems Engineering for Healthcare. Her educational focus is the development of innovative interprofessional graduate programs in nursing science and healthcare leadership that advance health and contribute to bold system change. She is a member of the Executive Committee of the California Action Coalition and a member of the Future of Nursing National Campaign Advisory Committee, Robert Wood Johnson Foundation, and Center to Champion Nursing in America.

Brenda Zierler, PhD, RN, FAAN, is a Professor in the School of Nursing at the University of Washington. She is Co-Director of the UW Center for Health Sciences Interprofessional Education and is Director of Faculty Development for UW Medicine's Institute for Simulation and Interprofessional Studies. Zierler is past-chair of the board for the American Interprofessional Health Collaborative and a member of the Institute of Medicine's Global Forum on Innovation in Health Professional Education. Zierler and Les Hall, MD, lead a national train-the-trainer interprofessional faculty development program funded by the Josiah Macy, Jr. Foundation. Zierler also leads three HRSA training grants: 1) technology enhanced IPE, 2) interprofessional collaborative practice for patients with advanced heart failure (AHF), and 3) an Education-Practice Partnership to Improve AHF Training and Outcomes for Rural and Underserved Populations.

Brenda Zierler
p. 67

Author Index

Index

INSTITUTE FOR GLOBAL HEALTHCARE LEADERSHIP

STTI's Institute for Global Healthcare Leadership developed two new leadership programs: The Experienced Global Leader Institute and the Emerging Global Leader Institute.

Launching in the fall of 2016, the Emerging Global Leader Institute will help prepare globally-aware healthcare leaders to:

1. Successfully participate in global healthcare ventures and networking.
2. Become a global thought and practice leader, locally and regionally.
3. Provide local and regional consultation to effectively meet dynamic contemporary global healthcare needs.
4. View healthcare issues from a global perspective.

Launching in 2018, the Experienced Global Leader Institute is designed to prepare experienced global healthcare leaders to:

1. Be global thought and practice leaders nationally and globally.
2. Successfully, lead, collaborate, and participate in global healthcare ventures.
3. Assume and effectively meet the global demands of critical healthcare leadership positions within their countries.
4. Provide national and global consultation to effectively meet dynamic contemporary global healthcare needs.

Go to http://ighl.nursingsociety.org/ for more information or to register.

INTERNATIONAL LEADERSHIP INSTITUTE
LEADERSHIP ACADEMIES

International Leadership Institute (ILI)

ILI focuses on developing nurse leaders through mentoring relationships, self-assessment, continuing nursing education, experiential learning, and professional development resources. STTI's four nurse leadership academies have changed lives, advanced careers, influenced organizational change, and ultimately improved patient care.

- **Nurse Faculty Leadership Academy (sponsored by Elsevier)**
  - Presented by STTI in partnership with The Elsevier Foundation, NFLA is an ideal experience for aspiring leaders in nursing education who have at least two, but no more than seven years of experience as full-time, nontenured faculty at a school of nursing. **Membership in STTI is not required.**

- **Maternal-Child Health Nurse Leadership Academy (sponsored by Johnson & Johnson)**
  - Presented by STTI in partnership with Johnson & Johnson, MCHNLA prepares nurses for effective interprofessional team leadership as they strive to improve the quality of healthcare for underserved childbearing women and children up to 5 years old. Previous MCHNLA fellows report a dramatic impact on their leadership skills and improved outcomes in their department, organization, and community. **Membership in STTI is not required.**

- **Maternal-Child Health Nurse Leadership Academy – Africa (sponsored by Johnson & Johnson)**
  - In cooperation with our funding partners Johnson & Johnson, MCHNLA Africa develops the leadership skills of maternal and child health nurses and midwives who work in a variety of healthcare settings.

- **Gerontological Nursing Leadership Academy (sponsored by Hill-Rom, Inc.)**
  - GNLA is an 18-month mentored leadership experience designed for master's-prepared nurses in diverse settings to lead interprofessional teams in the improvement of healthcare quality for older adults and their families. **Membership in STTI is not required.**

Go to <u>www.nursingsociety.org/leadership</u> for more information.

Sigma Theta Tau International /
Chamberlain College of Nursing

Center for Excellence
in Nursing Education

Sigma Theta Tau International/Chamberlain College of Nursing Center for Excellence in Nursing Education

The STTI/Chamberlain College of Nursing Center for Excellence in Nursing Education was established to advance excellence in nursing education. The center provides career and leadership development opportunities for academic nurse educators.

- **Experienced Nurse Faculty Leadership Academy**
  - This 12-month academy is for experienced nurse faculty with at least seven years in a full-time teaching role. Participants will increase their leadership acumen and develop and refine the skill set essential to success in a faculty leadership role.
- **Emerging Educational Administrator Institute**
  - This leadership development program is for new or aspiring nursing academic administrators. The program consists of online coursework, a face-to-face workshop, and completion of a leadership project.

- **Faculty Knowledge Skills Development Program**
  - This program offers professional development opportunities for new and experienced nurse faculty by utilizing a series of 15 webinars. These webinars are ideal for faculty orientation and continuing education requirements.
- **Faculty Professional Role Development Program**
  - These webinars will assist faculty in achieving career goals that lead to promotion and/or tenure. Topics include grantwriting, creating a professional portfolio, preparing for promotion on the clinical track, and more.

Go to www.nursingsociety.org/leadership for more information.

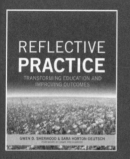
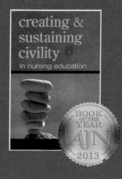

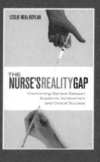

PRIORITY #2 Academic Progression

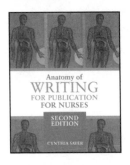

Anatomy of Writing for Publication for Nurses, Second Edition
By Cynthia L. Saver

ISBN: 9781938835421

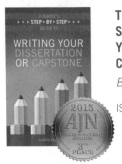

The Nurse's Step-by-Step Guide to Writing Your Dissertation or Capstone
By Karen M. Roush

ISBN: 9781940446080

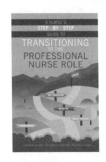

A Nurse's Step-by-Step Guide to Transitioning to the Professional Nurse Role
By Cynthia M. Thomas, Constance E. McIntosh, and Jennifer S. Mensik

ISBN: 9781940446226

Staff Educator's Guide to Professional Development
By Alvin D. Jeffrey, Anne Longo, Angela Nienaber

ISBN: 9781940446264

Accelerate Your Career in Nursing
By Janice Phillips and Janet Boivin

ISBN: 9781937554583

Take Charge of Your Nursing Career
By Lois Marshall

ISBN: 9781930538856

STTI books to help move nursing forward. Visit www.nursingknowledge.org/sttibooks for our full selection.

PRIORITY #3 Diversity

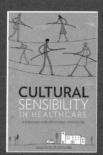

Cultural Sensibility

By Sally N. Ellis-Fletcher

ISBN: 9781937554958

The Nurse Manager's Guide to an Intergenerational Workforce

By Bonnie Clipper

ISBN: 9781937554750

Critical Conversations in Healthcare: Scripts and Techniques for Effective Interprofessional and Patient Communication

By Cheri Clancy

ISBN: 9781938835469

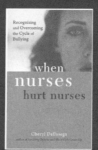

When Nurses Hurt Nurses: Recognizing and Overcoming the Cycle of Bullying

By Cheryl Dellasega

ISBN: 9781930476566

STTI books to help move nursing forward. Visit www.nursingknowledge.org/sttibooks for our full selection.

PRIORITY #4 Interprofessional Collaboration

Transforming Interprofessional Partnerships

By Riane Eisler and Teddie Potter

ISBN: 9781938835261

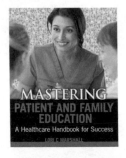

Mastering Patient and Family Education

By Lori C. Marshall

ISBN: 9781940446301

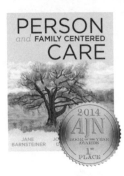

Person and Family Centered Care

By Jane Barnsteiner, Joanne Disch, and Mary K. Walton

ISBN: 9781938835070

Whole Person Caring: An Interprofessional Model for Healing and Wellness

By Lucia Thornton

ISBN: 9781937554996

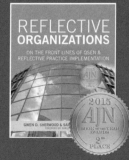

PRIORITY #6 Voices in Nursing

Your Path to the Boardroom
By Connie Curran

ISBN: 9781938835926

Claiming the Corner

Leading Valiantly in Healthcare
By Catherine Robin-son-Walker

ISBN: 9781937554835

Office: Executive Leadership Lessons for Nurses
By Connie Curran and Therese A. Fitzpatrick

ISBN: 9781937554354

The Nurse's Reality Shift
By Leslie J. Neal-Boylan

ISBN: 9781938835629

PRIORITY #7 Global Stewardship

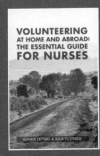

Volunteering at Home and Abroad

By Jeanne M. Leffers and Julia R. Plotnick

ISBN: 9781937554224

Nurse: A World of Care

By Peter Jaret, Marla K. Salmon, and Karen Kasmauski

ISBN: 9780981456508

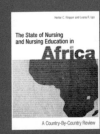

The State of Nursing and Nursing Education in Africa

By Hester Klopper and Leanna Uys

ISBN: 9781935476832

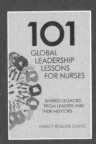

101 Global Leadership Lessons for Nurses

By Nancy Rollins Gantz

ISBN: 9781930538795

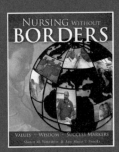

Nursing Without Borders

By Sharon M. Weinstein and Ann Marie T. Brooks

ISBN: 9781930538702

STTI books to help move nursing forward. Visit www.nursingknowledge.org/sttibooks for our full selection.

PRIORITY #8 Practice Authority

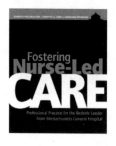

Fostering Nurse-Led Care

By Jeannette Ives Erickson, Dorothy Jones, and Marianne Ditomassi

ISBN: 9781935476306

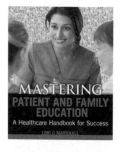

Mastering Patient and Family Education

By Lori C. Marshall

ISBN: 9781940446301

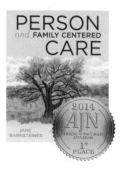

Person and Family Centered Care

By Jane Barnsteiner, Joanne Disch, and Mary K. Walton

ISBN: 9781938835070

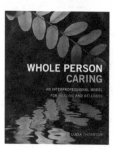

Whole Person Caring: An Interprofessional Model for Healing and Wellness

By Lucia Thornton

ISBN: 9781937554996

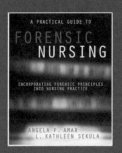

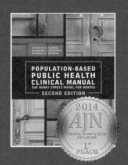
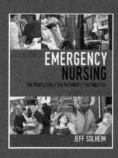

PRIORITY #10 Professional Handoff

The Career Handoff

By Kathy Malloch and Tim Porter-O'Grady

ISBN: 9781940446509

Leading Valiantly

By Catherine Robinson-Walker

ISBN: 9781937554835

Mentoring Today's Nurses

By Susan M. Baxley, Kristina S. Ibitayo, and Mary Lou Bond

ISBN: 9781937554910

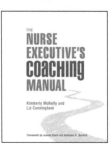

The Nurse Executive's Coaching Manual

By Kimberly McNally and Liz Cunningham

ISBN: 9781930538955

STTI books to help move nursing forward. Visit www.nursingknowledge.org/sttibooks for our full selection.

INTERNATIONAL LEADERSHIP INSTITUTE
LEADERSHIP ACADEMIES

International Leadership Institute (ILI)

ILI focuses on developing nurse leaders through mentoring relationships, self-assessment, continuing nursing education, experiential learning, and professional development resources. STTI's four nurse leadership academies have changed lives, advanced careers, influenced organizational change, and ultimately improved patient care.

- **Nurse Faculty Leadership Academy (sponsored by Elsevier)**
  - Presented by STTI in partnership with The Elsevier Foundation, NFLA is an ideal experience for aspiring leaders in nursing education who have at least two, but no more than seven years of experience as full-time, nontenured faculty at a school of nursing. **Membership in STTI is not required.**
- **Maternal-Child Health Nurse Leadership Academy (sponsored by Johnson & Johnson)**
  - Presented by STTI in partnership with Johnson & Johnson, MCHNLA prepares nurses for effective interprofessional team leadership as they strive to improve the quality of healthcare for underserved childbearing women and children up to 5 years old. Previous MCHNLA fellows report a dramatic impact on their leadership skills and improved outcomes in their department, organization, and community. **Membership in STTI is not required.**

- **Maternal-Child Health Nurse Leadership Academy – Africa (sponsored by Johnson & Johnson)**
  - In cooperation with our funding partners Johnson & Johnson, MCHNLA Africa develops the leadership skills of maternal and child health nurses and midwives who work in a variety of healthcare settings.
- **Gerontological Nursing Leadership Academy (sponsored by Hill-Rom, Inc.)**
  - GNLA is an 18-month mentored leadership experience designed for master's-prepared nurses in diverse settings to lead interprofessional teams in the improvement of healthcare quality for older adults and their families. **Membership in STTI is not required.**

Go to **www.nursingsociety.org/leadership** for more information.

Sigma Theta Tau International / Chamberlain College of Nursing

Center for Excellence in Nursing Education

Sigma Theta Tau International/Chamberlain College of Nursing Center for Excellence in Nursing Education

The STTI/Chamberlain College of Nursing Center for Excellence in Nursing Education was established to advance excellence in nursing education. The center provides career and leadership development opportunities for academic nurse educators.

- **Experienced Nurse Faculty Leadership Academy**
  - This 12-month academy is for experienced nurse faculty with at least seven years in a full-time teaching role. Participants will increase their leadership acumen and develop and refine the skill set essential to success in a faculty leadership role.
- **Emerging Educational Administrator Institute**
  - This leadership development program is for new or aspiring nursing academic administrators. The program consists of online coursework, a face-to-face workshop, and completion of a leadership project.

- **Faculty Knowledge Skills Development Program**
  - This program offers professional development opportunities for new and experienced nurse faculty by utilizing a series of 15 webinars. These webinars are ideal for faculty orientation and continuing education requirements.
- **Faculty Professional Role Development Program**
  - These webinars will assist faculty in achieving career goals that lead to promotion and/or tenure. Topics include grantwriting, creating a professional portfolio, preparing for promotion on the clinical track, and more.

Go to www.nursingsociety.org/leadership for more information.

INSTITUTE FOR GLOBAL HEALTHCARE LEADERSHIP

STTI's Institute for Global Healthcare Leadership developed two new leadership programs: The Experienced Global Leader Institute and the Emerging Global Leader Institute.

Launching in the fall of 2016, the Emerging Global Leader Institute will help prepare globally-aware healthcare leaders to:

1. Successfully participate in global healthcare ventures and networking.
2. Become a global thought and practice leader, locally and regionally.
3. Provide local and regional consultation to effectively meet dynamic contemporary global healthcare needs.
4. View healthcare issues from a global perspective.

Launching in 2018, the Experienced Global Leader Institute is designed to prepare experienced global healthcare leaders to:

1. Be global thought and practice leaders nationally and globally.
2. Successfully, lead, collaborate, and participate in global healthcare ventures.
3. Assume and effectively meet the global demands of critical healthcare leadership positions within their countries.
4. Provide national and global consultation to effectively meet dynamic contemporary global healthcare needs.

Go to http://ighl.nursingsociety.org/ for more information or to register.